A to Z
OF
Crochet

*Whatever you can do
or dream you can, begin it.
Boldness has genius,
power and magic in it.*

JOHANN WOLFGANG VON GOETHE

Martingale®
& COMPANY

A to Z of Crochet
© 2007 Country Bumpkin Publications

First published in Australia in 2007 by
Country Bumpkin Publications
916 South Road, Edwardstown
South Australia 5039, Australia
www.countrybumpkin.com.au

Editor: Sue Gardner
Assistant Editor: Lizzie Kulinski
Design and Layout: Lynton Grandison
Photography: Andrew Dunbar
Publisher: Margie Bauer

First published in U.S. in 2008 by
Martingale & Company®
19021 120th Ave. NE, Ste. 102
Bothell, WA 98011-9511 USA
ShopMartingale.com

ISBN: 978-1-56477-998-4

Printed in China
18 17 16 15   17 16 15

Mission Statement
Dedicated to providing quality products
and service to inspire creativity.

Contents

Contents

Yarns

Virtually anything from strips of fabric, wire, and string to knitting yarns, embroidery threads, ribbons, and anything in between can be used for crochet. Of course, yarns specially made for crochet are the easiest to use, but the effects created when using something different can be worth the added difficulty.

Yarns designed specifically for crochet are generally smooth and firm and it is best to use a yarn of this type when learning a new technique.

Here are a few points to consider when selecting your yarn:

> Mercerized cotton threads are generally stronger than other cotton threads. The process of mercerizing the cotton also adds a lovely sheen to it.

> Woolen and wool-blend yarns are nice to work with and have a certain amount of stretch that makes it easier to insert your hook.

> Natural linen yarns create a crisp, neat, durable fabric but it can sometimes be quite stiff. If linen yarn is blended with something else, it is generally softer.

> Acrylic and nylon yarns are usually inexpensive but are more likely to pill than other yarns.

> Loosely woven yarns have a tendency to split when crocheting, making it difficult to pick up stitches.

> Hairy, heavily textured and furry yarns will disguise the structure of your stitches and can make it more difficult to maintain an even gauge to your work. They can also be difficult to unravel if you have a mistake to fix.

> Silk has a wonderful luster and is very comfortable to wear, keeping you warm when the weather is cool and cool when the weather is warm. However, it is expensive and less resilient than many other yarns.

> Good-quality blended yarns usually retain the best properties of their component fibers.

> Dark colors can make it difficult to see stitches unless you are working in particularly good light.

If you purchase yarn by the hank, you will find it easier to work with if you wind it into a ball.

When using a yarn different from the one recommended in the pattern, it is doubly important to crochet a gauge swatch and check your hook size. Try to choose a yarn that is a similar weight to the original yarn.

Hooks

Standard crochet hooks come in a wide range of sizes, colors and materials. They can be made of aluminium, steel, wood, bamboo, and plastic. Antique hooks were made of wood, bone, ivory, Bakelite, and resin.

Steel hooks are generally used when working with fine cotton and linen threads. Aluminium and plastic hooks are the most commonly available hooks and are generally used with a wide variety of yarns.

Your pattern will recommend the size of the hook you need for a particular project (although you may vary this depending on your gauge; see page 8). Apart from size, the most important thing you need to consider when selecting a hook is how comfortable it is for you to hold. Try handling several brands before you make your purchase.

Afghan hooks have a long, cylindrical shaft and a knob at one end to prevent stitches from falling off. They are sometimes known as "tricot needles."

The hook needs to be long enough to hold all the stitches across the entire width of your piece.

Double-ended hooks connected with a flexible plastic tube, much like circular knitting needles, are also suitable for afghan crochet.

Other tools and equipment

Measuring tools

A flexible tape measure that shows both imperial and metric measurements on the same side is the most useful. However, with use, these tapes can stretch and therefore become inaccurate, so if your tape measure is showing signs of wear, it is worth purchasing a new one.

A metal or plastic ruler approximately 12" (30 cm) long is also useful for measuring gauge swatches.

Needles

Use a needle with a large eye and blunt tip so you do not split your crochet stitches. Tapestry needles are the perfect choice and they come in sizes ranging from 18–28. Yarn darners are longer than tapestry needles and are also excellent choices.

Pins

Choose long pins with large heads so that you do not lose them in your work. Glass-headed pins are the most versatile as they can be used for blocking as well as pinning seams together.

Sizes: conversion chart

Sizes given do not always correspond exactly, so use this chart as a guide only.

Aluminum and plastic hooks			Steel hooks		
Metric size	UK	US sizes	Metric size	UK sizes	US sizes
2.00 mm	14	–	0.60 mm	6	12
2.25 mm	13	B-1	–	5½	11
2.50 mm	12	–	0.75 mm	5	10
2.75 mm	–	C-2	–	4½	–
3.00 mm	11	–	1.00 mm	4	9
3.25 mm	10	D-3	–	3½	–
3.50 mm	9	E-4	1.25 mm	3	–
3.75 mm	–	F-5	1.50 mm	2½	8
4.00 mm	8	G-6	1.65 mm	–	7
4.50 mm	7	7	1.80 mm	2	6
5.00 mm	6	H-8	1.90 mm	1½	5
5.50 mm	5	I-9	2.00 mm	1	4
6.00 mm	4	J-10	2.10 mm	1/0 or 0	3
6.50 mm	3	K-10½	2.25 mm	–	2
7.00 mm	2	–	2.50 mm	2/0 or 00	–
8.00 mm	1	L-11	2.75 mm	–	1
9.00 mm	0	M/N-13	3.00 mm	3/0 or 000	–
10.00 mm	00	N/P-15	3.25 mm	–	0
12.00 mm	–	–	3.50 mm	–	00
15.00 mm	–	P/Q			

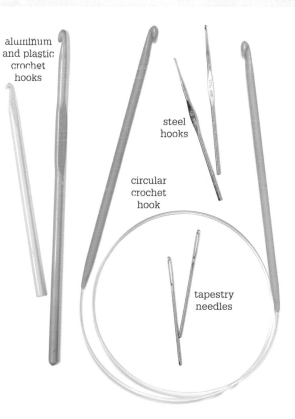

aluminum and plastic crochet hooks

steel hooks

circular crochet hook

tapestry needles

Scissors

A pair of small, sharp, pointed scissors is recommended for cutting yarn and trimming off tails.

Stitch markers

Stitch markers do exactly what their name suggests. Commercially made markers come in a variety of shapes and colors but all have a narrow split so that they can be slipped on and off your work easily. A safety pin also makes an adequate stitch marker.

Specialty items

If you want to try your hand at broomstick crochet, you will need a large knitting needle. The length of the needle will limit the width of your piece. If you cannot find a needle of a suitable diameter and length, use a length of wooden dowel. Sharpen one end into a point and sand it smooth with fine sandpaper.

For hairpin crochet, you will need a hairpin tool. These can be purchased from specialty needlework and knitting shops. The most versatile tools have several holes in them so you can adjust the width of your work.

Gauge

Gauge is the key to having your crocheted pieces turn out the correct size. Even a small difference in gauge will alter the finished size of your piece.

Gauge is affected by the way you hold the yarn and hook, the type of yarn you are using, the size of the hook, and the pattern of the stitches.

How to measure gauge

Using your planned yarn, hook, and the main stitch pattern for your piece, work a swatch that is 6" to 8" (15 to 20 cm) square. Block the swatch following the instructions on page 149. Lay the swatch on a flat surface and measure 4" (10 cm) across the middle of the swatch, making sure you follow a row carefully. Mark with two pins. Count the number of stitches between the two pins. Repeat this process vertically, counting the number of rows. Compare your findings with those in the pattern.

Some designs will state the gauge as a number of pattern repeats. In this case, count pattern repeats, rather than stitches.

Altering gauge

If you have more rows or stitches within the 4" (10 cm) area than the pattern indicated, it means your gauge is too firm. Change to a larger hook and crochet another swatch.

If you have fewer rows or stitches within the 4" (10 cm) area than the pattern indicated, it means your gauge is too loose. Change to a smaller hook and crochet another swatch.

While this may seem tedious, it is well worth taking the time to achieve the right gauge before beginning your project.

Reading patterns and charts

Abbreviations and symbols

Crochet patterns generally use abbreviations to describe the stitches you need to make so they do not become too lengthy. You will also find crochet instructions presented as charts. This is particularly so for lacy designs and patterns that originate in Europe (England being the exception). In a chart, each stitch is represented by a symbol.

stitch	abbreviation	symbol
Bobble	bo	
Chain stitch	ch	O
Cluster	cl	⋔
Single crochet	sc	+
Single crochet two together	sc2tog	
Single crochet three together	sc3tog	
Triple crochet	tr	⸶
Half double crochet	hdc	T
Picot	p	
Popcorn	pc	
Front-post double crochet	FPdc	⌡
Back-post double crochet	BPdc	⌐
Slip stitch	sl st	●
Double crochet	dc	⸶
Double triple crochet	dtr	⸷
Alternate	alt	
Turning chain	tch	
Begin/beginning	beg	
Between	bet	
Continue	cont	
Contrast color	CC	
Decrease	dec	
Follow/following	foll	
Increase	inc	
Pattern	patt	
Previous	prev	
Repeat	rep	

stitch	abbreviation	symbol
Right side	RS	
Round	rnd	
Double crochet two together	dc2tog	
Double crochet three together	dc3tog	
Skip	sk	
Space	sp	
Stitch	st	
Stitches	sts	
Together	tog	
Wrong side	WS	
Yarn over	yo	

Instructions for filet crochet are also presented as charts but these are different from those above. A square grid is used. The open spaces represent filet spaces, and the filled-in spaces represent blocks. The way the spaces are filled will vary but the result is the same.

US/UK terminology

When following a pattern, always check its origin, because you'll find that some of the terminology is different in American patterns and instructions compared to English and Australian patterns and instructions. This table will help you make the conversion.

American terms	Aust/English terms	symbol
Single crochet	Double crochet	+
Extended single crochet	Extended double crochet	†
Half double crochet	Half treble	T
Double crochet	Treble	⸶
Triple crochet	Double treble	⸷
Double triple crochet	Triple treble	⸷
Afghan stitch	Tunisian stitch	
Gauge	Tension	
Skip	Miss	

There are several different ways to hold both the hook and the yarn. Experiment and choose the way that feels most comfortable for you and gives you the best results.

Holding the Yarn and Hook

Right-handed hook holds

  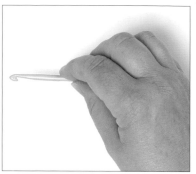

1. Hold the hook in the same manner as you would a pencil, keeping the tips of your thumb and forefinger in the middle of the flat section.

2. Hold the hook in the same manner as you would hold a knife, again gripping the flat section with the tips of your thumb and middle finger.

3. Hold the hook in the same manner as you would a violin bow. Keep the tips of your thumb and index finger in the middle of the flat section.

Right-handed yarn holds

1A. Weave the yarn from the ball through the fingers of your left hand as shown, making sure the end of the yarn is at the top.

1B. While holding the hook with your right hand, hold the slipknot with your left thumb and middle finger.

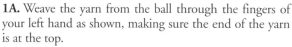

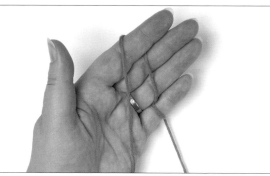 

2A. Take the end of the yarn across your left palm and over your index finger, across your second and third fingers, and then around your little finger.

2B. While holding the hook with your right hand, hold the slipknot with your left thumb and middle finger.

Left-handed hook holds

1. Hold the hook in the same manner as you would a pencil, keeping the tips of your thumb and index finger in the middle of the flat section.

2. Hold the hook in the same manner as you would hold a knife, again gripping the flat section with the tips of your thumb and middle finger.

3. Hold the hook in the same manner as you would a violin bow. Keep the tips of your thumb and index finger in the middle of the flat section.

Left-handed yarn holds

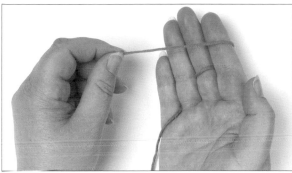 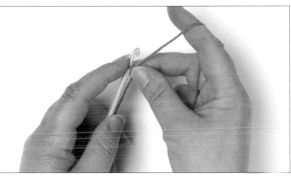

1A. Weave the yarn from the ball through the fingers of your right hand as shown, making sure the end of the yarn is at the top.

1B. While holding the hook with your left hand, hold the slipknot with your right thumb and middle finger.

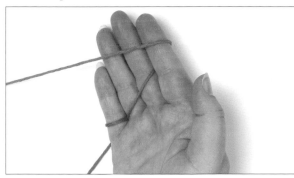 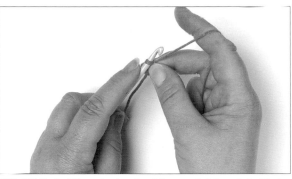

2A. Take the end of the yarn across your right palm and over your index finger, across your second and third fingers, and then around your little finger.

2B. While holding the hook with your left hand, hold the slipknot with your right thumb and middle finger.

The first loop of any piece of crochet is made with a slipknot. It is not counted as a stitch.

Slipknot: Method 1 In this method the knot slides from the tail end of the yarn.

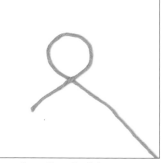

1. Loop the tail end of the yarn in a clockwise direction to form a circle.

2. Pick up this loop with one hand and take the tail end of the yarn, from back to front, through the circle to form a second loop.

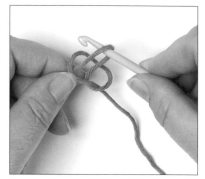

3. Take your hook through the second loop.

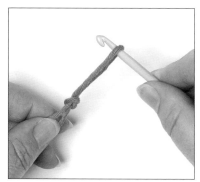

4. Hold both ends of the yarn with your left hand and pull the hook upward to tighten the knot.

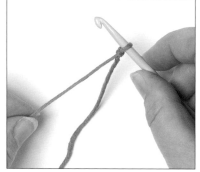

5. Tighten the loop around your hook by pulling on the tail end of the yarn.

Method 2 In this method the knot slides from the ball end of the yarn.

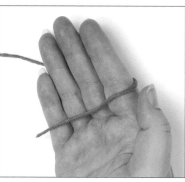

1. With your palm facing you, lay the yarn across your fingers as shown.

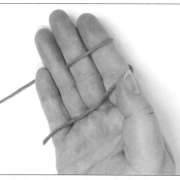

2. Wrap the yarn from the ball around your first two fingers.

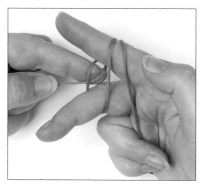

3. Separate your fingers slightly. Take the yarn, from back to front, through the loop formed.

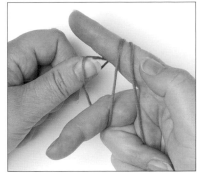

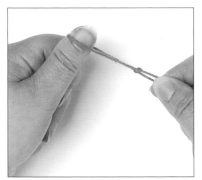

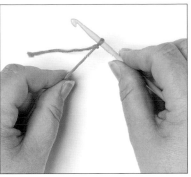

4. Pick up the new loop of yarn with your thumb.

5. Hold both ends of the yarn with your right hand and pull your thumb upwards to tighten the knot.

6. Place the loop on your hook and tighten by pulling on the ball end of the yarn.

Basic Stitches: Chain Stitch (ch)

Foundation chain Working a string of chain stitches is the equivalent of casting on in knitting.

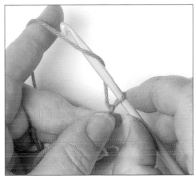

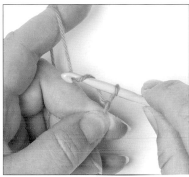

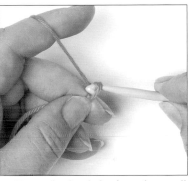

1. Take the yarn from the ball, from back to front, over the hook.

2. Catch this section of yarn in the barb of the hook.

3. Draw the hook backward to pull the yarn through the slipknot.

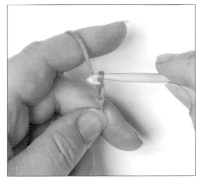

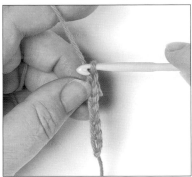

4. A new loop forms on the hook and the previous loop drops below it.

5. Repeat steps 1–4 to form a second chain stitch.

6. Continue working chain stitches in the same manner until you have enough to cover the desired width of your piece.

From the beginning

Turning chain

Chain stitches are also used to move to the beginning position for the next row or round of stitches.

1. When working single crochet stitch, work one turning chain.

2. When working half double crochet, work two turning chain stitches.

HINTS
Chain stitch

If you crochet very tightly, work an extra turning chain so that the edges of your work do not become too tight.

When counting the number of chains you have worked, do not count the slipknot or the loop on the hook. Either count the Vs on the front of the chain or the bumps along the center on the back.

To help maintain an even gauge, keep changing your grip on the worked chains so you are always holding them near the hook.

3. When working double crochet, work three turning chain stitches.

4. When working triple crochet stitch, work four turning chain stitches.

Slip Stitch (sl st)

Slip stitch is used to join ends into a circle or to invisibly move to a different position on your work.

HINTS
Slip stitch

Take care not to work slip stitches too tightly as you can pucker your crocheted fabric.

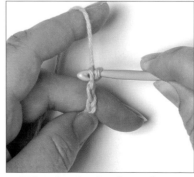

1. Take the hook, from front to back, through the top loop of the foundation chain.

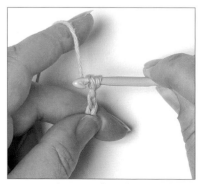

2. Wrap the yarn, from back to front, over the hook. Catch this section of yarn in the barb of the hook.

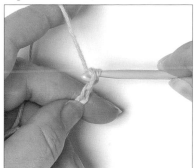

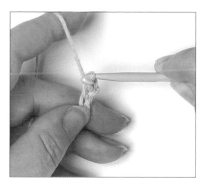

3. Draw the hook backward to pull the yarn through both loops on the hook.

4. A new loop remains on the hook.

5. To move to a different position, repeat steps 1–4 through each stitch until you reach the desired position.

Single Crochet Stitch (sc)

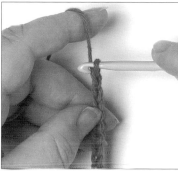

1. Work the required number of chain stitches for the width of your piece and then one more chain (this is the turning chain).

2. First row. Take the hook, from front to back, through the second chain from the hook.

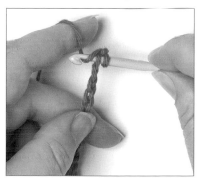

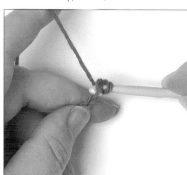

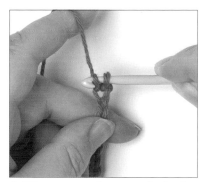

3. Take the yarn from back to front over the hook. This is known as a yarn over.

4. Catch this section of yarn in the barb of the hook. Draw the hook backward to pull the yarn through the loop of the chain stitch.

5. There are two loops on the hook.

From the beginning

15

6. Wrap the yarn over the hook in the same manner as before.

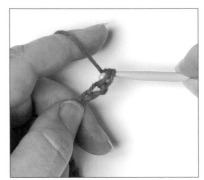

7. Draw the hook backward to pull the yarn through both loops on the hook.

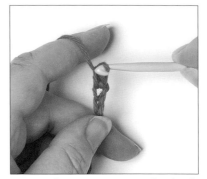

8. One loop remains on the hook and the stitch is completed.

9. Take the hook, from front to back, through the next chain.

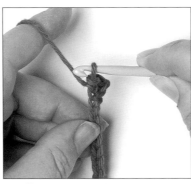

10. Repeat steps 3–8.

11. Continue to the end of the chains, working a stitch into each one.

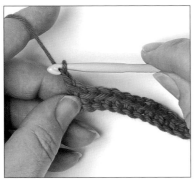

12. Work a single chain stitch (this is the turning chain).

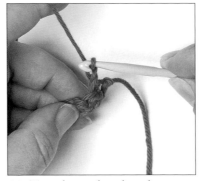

13. Turn the crocheted work.

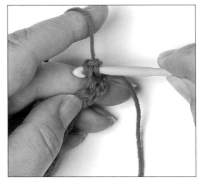

14. Subsequent rows. Take the hook, from front to back, behind the top of the last single crochet in the previous row. This looks like the V on the front of a chain stitch.

15. Repeat steps 3–8.

16. Continue in the same manner to the end of the row, working a stitch into the top of each single crochet of the previous row. Do not work into the turning chain of the previous row.

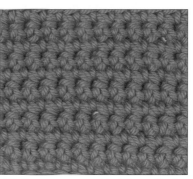

17. Repeat steps 12–16 until the work is the required length. Fasten off following the instructions on page 24.

Half Double Crochet Stitch (hdc)

This stitch is halfway between the single crochet stitch and the double crochet stitch in height.

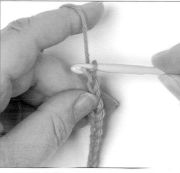

1. Work the required number of chain stitches for the width of your piece and then two more chains (these make the turning chain).

2. First row. Wrap the yarn, from back to front, over the hook. This is known as a yarn over.

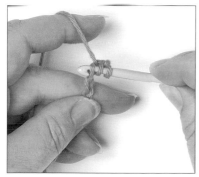

3. Take the hook, from front to back, through the third chain from the hook. There are three loops on the hook.

4. Take the yarn, from back to front, over the hook.

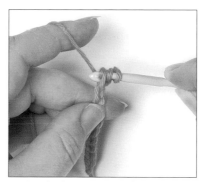

5. Catch this section of yarn in the barb of the hook. Draw the hook backward to pull the yarn through the loop of the chain stitch.

From the beginning

17

Half double crochet stitch / continued

6. Three loops remain on the hook.

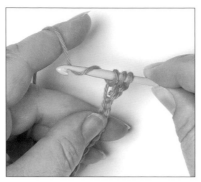

7. Wrap the yarn over the hook in the same manner as before.

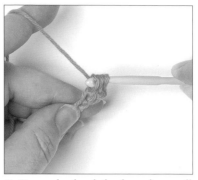

8. Draw the hook backward to pull the yarn through all three loops on the hook.

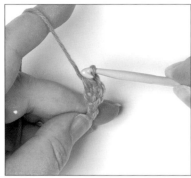

9. One loop remains on the hook and the stitch is completed.

10. Working through the next chain, repeat steps 2–9 to form a second stitch.

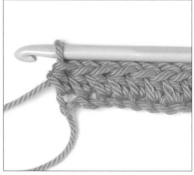

11. Continue to the end of the chains, working a stitch into each one.

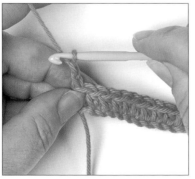

12. Work two chain stitches (this is the turning chain).

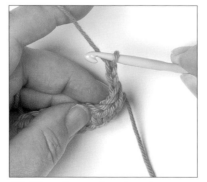

13. Turn the crocheted work.

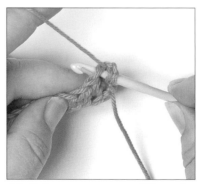

14. Subsequent rows. Wrap the yarn as before and take the hook, from front to back, behind the top of the second to last half double crochet in the previous row. This looks like the V on the front of a chain stitch.

From the beginning

15. Repeat steps 2–9.

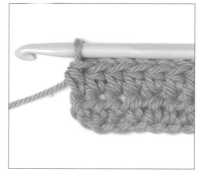

16. Continue working stitches in the same manner to the end of the row, working a stitch into the top of each half double crochet of the previous row and one into the top of the turning chain of the previous row.

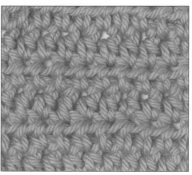

17. Repeat steps 12–16 until the work is the required length. Fasten off following the instructions on page 24.

Double Crochet Stitch (dc)

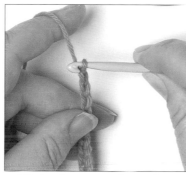

1. Work the required number of chain stitches for the width of your piece and then three more chains (these make the turning chain).

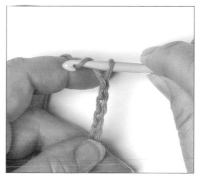

2. First row. Wrap the yarn, from back to front, over the hook. This is known as a yarn over.

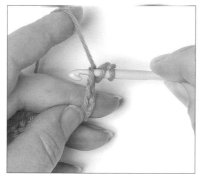

3. Take the hook, from front to back, through the fourth chain from the hook. There are now three loops on the hook.

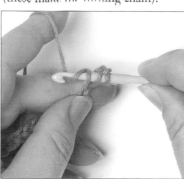

4. Again, take the yarn, from back to front, over the hook.

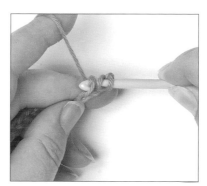

5. Catch this section of yarn in the barb of the hook. Draw the hook backward to pull the yarn through the loop of the chain stitch.

Double crochet stitch / continued

6. Three loops remain on the hook.

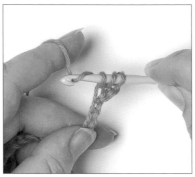

7. Wrap the yarn over the hook in the same manner as before.

8. Draw the hook backward to pull the yarn through the first two loops on the hook.

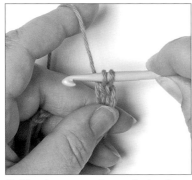

9. Two loops remain on the hook.

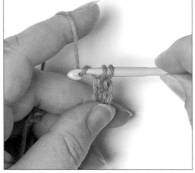

10. Wrap the yarn over the hook in the same manner as before.

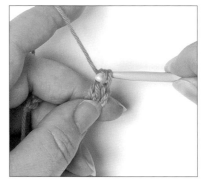

11. Draw the hook backward to pull the yarn through both of the loops on the hook.

12. One loop remains on the hook and the stitch is completed.

13. Working through the next chain, repeat steps 2–12 to form a second stitch.

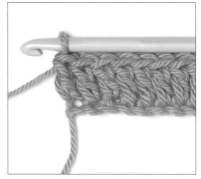

14. Continue to the end of the chains, working a stitch into each one.

From the beginning

20

15. Work three chain stitches (this is the turning chain).

16. Turn the crocheted work.

17. Subsequent rows. Wrap yarn as before and take hook, from front to back, behind top of second to last dc in the previous row. This looks like the V on the front of a chain stitch.

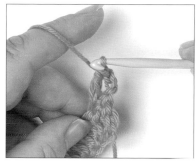

18. Repeat steps 4–12.

19. Continue in the same manner to the end of the row, working a stitch into the top of each dc stitch of the previous row and one into the top of the turning chain of the previous row.

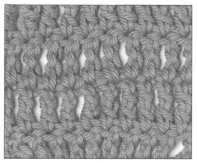

20. Continue working rows in the same manner until the work is the required length. Fasten off following the instructions on page 24.

Triple Crochet Stitch (trc)

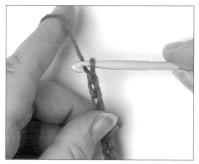

1. Work the required number of chain stitches for the width of your piece and then four more chains (these make the turning chain).

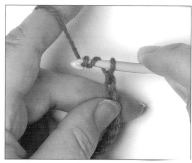

2. First row. Wrap the yarn, from back to front, over the hook twice. This is known as a yarn over.

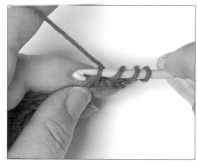

3. Take the hook, from front to back, through the fifth chain from the hook. There are now four loops on the hook.

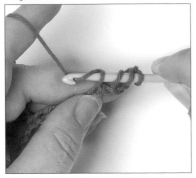

4. Again, take the yarn, from back to front, over the hook.

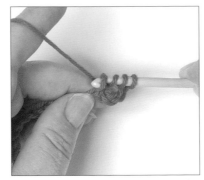

5. Catch this section of yarn in the barb of the hook. Draw the hook backward to pull the yarn through the loop of the chain stitch.

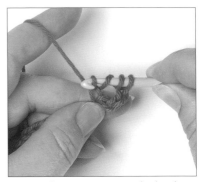

6. Four loops remain on the hook.

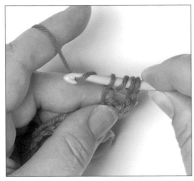

7. Wrap the yarn over the hook in the same manner as before.

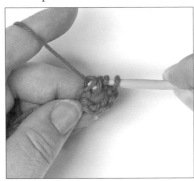

8. Draw the hook backward to pull the yarn through the first two loops on the hook.

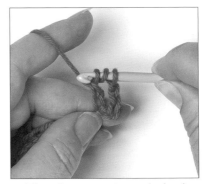

9. Three loops remain on the hook.

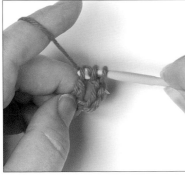

10. Wrap the yarn over the hook in the same manner as before. Draw the hook backward to pull the yarn through the first two loops on the hook.

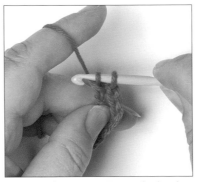

11. Two loops remain on the hook.

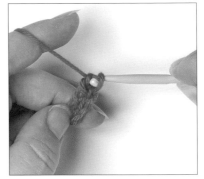

12. Wrap the yarn over the hook in the same manner as before. Draw the hook backward to pull the yarn through both of the loops on the hook.

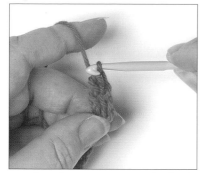

13. One loop remains on the hook and the stitch is completed

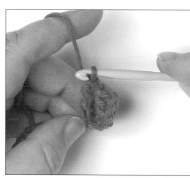

14. Working through the next chain, repeat steps 2–13 to form a second stitch.

15. Continue to the end of the chains, working a stitch into each one.

16. Work four chain stitches (this is the turning chain).

17. Turn the crocheted work.

18. Subsequent rows. Wrap the yarn twice as before and take the hook, from front to back, behind the top of the second to last triple crochet in the previous row. This looks like the V on the front of a chain stitch.

19. Repeat steps 4–13.

20. Continue working stitches in the same manner to end of row, working a stitch into the top of each triple crochet of the previous row and into the top of the turning chain of the previous row.

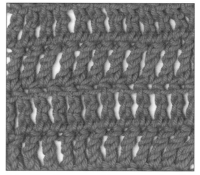

21. Continue working rows in the same manner until the work is the required length. Fasten off following the instructions on page 24.

When you have finished crocheting your piece, use this method to fasten off the yarn.

Fastening Off Yarn Securing the yarn

1. Leaving a 6" (15 cm) tail, cut off the excess yarn.

2. Bring the yarn, from back to front, over the hook and catch it in the barb.

3. Draw the hook backward to pull a loop of yarn through the loop on the hook (you are making a chain stitch).

4. Continue pulling the yarn until it is completely through.

5. Hold the last chain stitch firmly and tug on the tail of yarn to tighten.

Weaving in the tail of yarn at the upper edge

1. Thread the tail of yarn onto a tapestry needle.

2. On the wrong side of the crocheted fabric, take the needle, from bottom to top, behind the first loop of yarn on the upper edge.

3. Pull the yarn through.

Weaving in the tail of yarn at the upper edge / continued

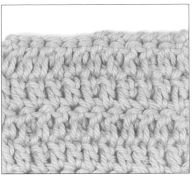

4. Take the needle behind the second loop of yarn on the upper edge.

5. Pull the yarn through as before. Weave the yarn through several more loops in the same manner.

6. Trim the excess yarn close to the fabric.

Weaving in the tail of yarn in the middle of the fabric

If different colors are used, weave the tail behind stitches of the same color.

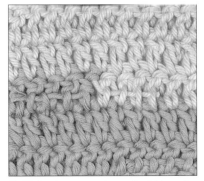

1. Thread one tail of yarn into a tapestry needle.

2. With the wrong side of the crocheted fabric facing you, take the needle through several stitches in the same row that the tail begins in.

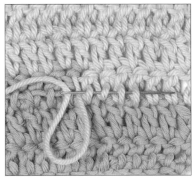

3. Pull the yarn through. Trim the excess yarn close to the fabric.

4. Thread the remaining tail into the needle and take it through several stitches on the wrong side of the fabric in the opposite direction to the first tail.

5. Pull the yarn through. Trim the excess yarn close to the fabric.

Weaving in the tail of yarn at the lower edge

1. Thread the tail of yarn into a tapestry needle.

2. With the wrong side of the crocheted fabric facing you, take the needle, through several stitches in the first row.

3. Pull the yarn through. Trim the excess yarn close to the fabric.

Joining Yarns
Joining in the middle of a row

1. Work the last stitch before the new yarn is to begin, until it has two loops on the hook.

2. Wrap the new yarn, from back to front, around the hook in the same way as for previous stitches.

3. Draw the hook backward, pulling a loop of the new yarn through the two loops and onto the hook.

4. Continue stitching with the new yarn.

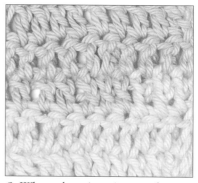

5. When the piece is complete or after several rows, fasten off the tails of thread following the instructions on page 25.

Joining at the end of a row

1. Partially work the last stitch of the previous row before the new yarn is to begin. Work the stitch until it has two loops on the hook.

2. Wrap the new yarn, from back to front, around the hook in the same way as for previous stitches.

3. Draw the hook backward, pulling a loop of the new yarn through the two loops and onto the hook.

4. Work your turning chain and then turn your work. Lay the two tails of yarn along the top of the previous row.

5. Take the hook through the first stitch in the usual manner.

6. Work the stitch in the usual manner, enclosing the tails within the stitch.

7. Work several more stitches, enclosing the tails in the same manner.

8. Trim the tails of yarn close to the last worked stitch.

9. Continue to the end of the row.

Joining with slip stitch This method will work no matter what stitch you are using.

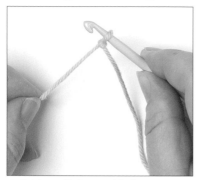

1. Make a slipknot with the new yarn and place it on the hook.

2. Take the hook, from front to back, through the stitch.

3. Take the new yarn, from back to front, around the hook.

4. Draw the hook backward and pull the wrapped yarn through both the first stitch and slipknot.

5. Continue across the row with the new yarn.

Sewing ends together

1. Thread the tail of the new yarn into a tapestry needle. Stretch the tail of the old yarn over your fingers. Beginning at the end of the tail, work running stitches through the old yarn for approximately 3⅛" (8 cm).

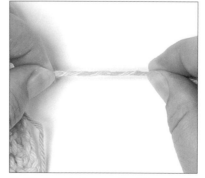

2. Unthread the needle. Very gently pull both yarns until the stitched section is about the same thickness as one strand of yarn.

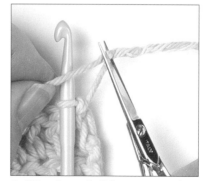

3. Trim the end of the yarn very close to the stitching.

Shaping

Single increase within a row

1. Stitch to the position of the increase. At this position, work a stitch into the next stitch of the previous row as before.

2. Take your hook through exactly the same stitch in the previous row.

3. Work a second stitch in exactly the same manner as the first stitch.

Double increase within a row

1. Stitch to the position of the increase. At this position, work a stitch into the next stitch of the previous row as before. Take your hook through exactly the same stitch in the previous row.

2. Work a second stitch into the same stitch of the previous row in exactly the same manner as the first stitch.

3. Work a third stitch through exactly the same stitch of the previous row.

Single increase within a row   Double increase within a row   Increases at the ends of rows

Increasing at the end of a row Any number of stitches can be added in this way.

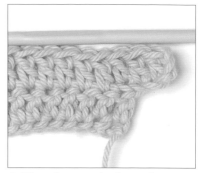

1. Stitch to the end of the row. Work a single chain for each additional stitch required plus your turning chain.

2. Turn your work. Stitch across the new section in the same manner as for a foundation chain and then continue across your previous stitches.

3. The photograph above shows an increase of two stitches.

Increasing at the other end of a row Any number of stitches can be added in this way.

1. Work almost to the end of the row where the increase will occur. Leave approximately five or six stitches unworked. Remove your hook.

2. Join a new yarn to the last stitch in the previous row (see page 28).

3. Work a single chain for each additional stitch required.

4. Fasten off the new yarn.

5. Work the five or six unworked stitches and then work across the new section in the same manner as for a foundation chain.

6. Turn your work and continue working as before.

Decreasing by skipping a stitch

This method works with all stitches but it does leave holes in the fabric.

1. Work to the position of the decrease. Skip one stitch and take the hook, from front to back, through the next stitch. (Remember to wrap the yarn first if working a double crochet stitch.)

2. Work the stitch in the same manner as your previous stitches.

Decreasing one single crochet within a row (sc2tog)

1. Work to the position of the decrease. Take the hook, from front to back, through the next stitch.

2. Wrap the yarn, from back to front, over the hook and pull the loop through the picked-up stitch. There are two loops on the hook.

3. Take the hook, from front to back, through the next stitch.

4. Wrap the yarn, from back to front, over the hook and pull the loop through the picked-up stitch. There are three loops on the hook.

5. Wrap the yarn, from back to front, over the hook and pull the loop through all three loops on the hook.

Decreasing two single crochet stitches within a row (sc3tog)

1. Work to the position of the decrease and work steps 1–4 on page 31.

2. Take the hook, from front to back, through the next stitch. Wrap the yarn and pull the loop through the picked-up stitch as before. There are four loops on the hook.

3. Wrap the yarn, from back to front, over the hook and pull the loop through all four loops on the hook.

Decreasing one double crochet within a row (dc2tog)

1. Work to the position of the decrease. Wrap the yarn, from back to front, over the hook and take the hook, from front to back, through the next stitch.

2. Wrap the yarn, from back to front, over the hook and pull the loop through the picked-up stitch. There are three loops on the hook.

3. Wrap the yarn as before and pull the loop through the first two loops on the hook.

4. Wrap the yarn, from back to front, over the hook and take the hook, from front to back, through the next stitch.

5. Repeat steps 2–3. You will have three loops on the hook.

6. Wrap the yarn as before and pull it through all three loops on the hook.

Decreasing two double crochet stitches within a row (dc3tog)

Decreasing by single crocheting three together

1. Work to the position of the decrease and work steps 1–5 on page 32.

2. Wrap yarn and take hook, from front to back, through next stitch. Wrap yarn and pull loop through picked-up stitch, leaving five loops on hook.

Decreasing by double crocheting two together

3. Wrap the yarn, from back to front, over the hook and pull the loop through the first two loops on the hook. Four loops remain on the hook.

4. Wrap the yarn as before and pull it through all four loops on the hook.

Stepped decreasing at the end of a row

Slip stitches are used to create stepped decreases.

Decreasing by double crocheting three together

1. Work the required number of rows without decreasing. Turn your work without working any turning chains.

2. Take the hook, from front to back, through the first stitch of the previous row and wrap the yarn, from back to front, over the hook.

3. Pull the wrap through both the stitch and loop on the hook.

4. One loop remains on the hook.

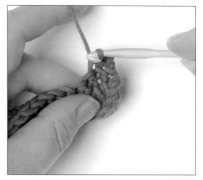

5. Take the hook through the next stitch of the previous row and complete the slip stitch as before.

6. Continue working slip stitches across the row until you have decreased the required number of stitches.

7. Work the required number of turning chain for your stitch (but do not turn your work).

8. Work stitches across the row.

9. If you wish to decrease at the opposite end, stop before the end of the row, leaving the required number of stitches unworked.

10. Work your turning chain, turn your work, and begin the next row.

Sloped decreasing at the end of a row

This method works for stitches in the double or triple crochet family. We have used triple crochet.

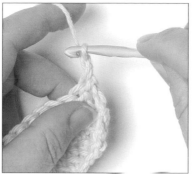

1. Work the required number of rows without decreasing. Work one turning chain and turn your work.

2. Work a single crochet into the first stitch of the previous row.

HINTS Shaping

If you need to increase at the same position in subsequent rows, place a marker, such as a piece of contrasting yarn, at the position where your increasing begins.

To maintain a neat edge to your work, do not work an increase into the first or last stitches. Instead, use the second or second-to-last stitches.

The number of stitches used to create a slope will depend on the stitch you are working with. A row of half double crochet will require one single crochet for the slope. A row of double crochet will require one single crochet and one half double crochet for the slope. A row of triple crochet will require one single crochet, one half double crochet, and one double crochet for the slope.

3. Work a half double crochet into the second stitch of the previous row. (If you are working a fabric of half double crochet, continue working stitches across the row at this point.)

4. Work a double crochet into the third stitch of the previous row. (If you are working a fabric of double crochet, continue working stitches across the row at this point.)

5. Work a triple crochet into the fourth stitch of the previous row. Continue working stitches across the row.

6. To decrease at the other end, work the starting stitches in the reverse order.

Bobbles use more yarn than most other stitches and are usually worked in wrong-side rows.

Surround bobbles with shorter stitches, such as single crochet, to make them stand out more from the background.

Bobbles

Bobbles are usually worked with three to five double crochet stitches. They are worked into the same stitch at the base and closed at the top.

Bobble with five double crochet stitches

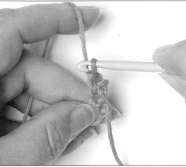

1. On a wrong-side row, stitch to the position for the bobble.

2. Wrap the yarn, from back to front, over the hook.

3. Take the hook, from front to back, through the top of the next stitch of the previous row.

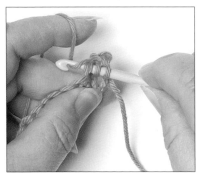

4. Again, wrap the yarn, from back to front, over the hook.

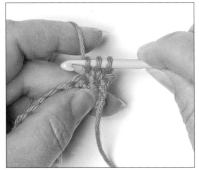

5. Draw the hook backward to pull the loop through the top of the stitch. There are three loops on the hook.

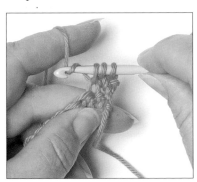

6. Again, wrap the yarn, from back to front, over the hook.

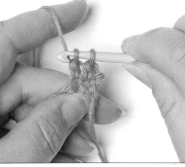

7. Draw the hook backward to pull the loop through the first two loops on the hook. Two loops remain on the hook.

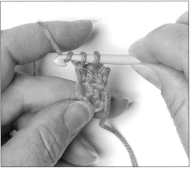

8. Wrap the yarn, from back to front, over the hook.

Bobble with five double crochet stitches / continued

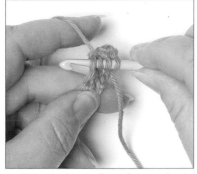

9. Take the hook, from front to back, through the top of the same stitch as before.

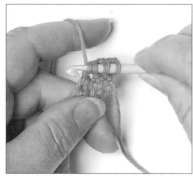

10. Wrap the yarn, from back to front, over the hook. Draw the hook backward to pull the yarn through the top of the stitch of the previous row. There are four loops on the hook.

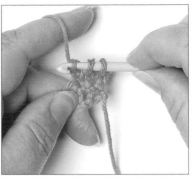

11. Repeat steps 6–7. You will have three loops on the hook.

12. Following steps 9–11, work three more stitches in the same manner. You will have six loops on the hook.

13. Wrap the yarn, from back to front, over the hook.

14. Draw the hook backward to pull the yarn through all the loops on the hook.

15. Wrap the yarn, from back to front, over the hook.

16. Draw the hook backward to pull the yarn through the remaining loop on the hook and secure the bobble.

17. Continue stitching to the end of the row, working the bobbles between your other stitches.

Bullion Stitches

This stitch is reminiscent of the bullion knots so popular in surface embroidery.

1. Stitch to the position for the bullion.

2. Wrap the yarn, from back to front, over the hook seven times.

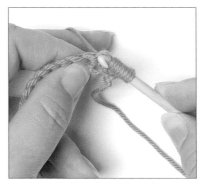

3. Take the hook, from front to back, through the top of the next stitch of the previous row.

4. Again, wrap the yarn, from back to front, over the hook.

5. Draw the hook backward to pull the loop through the top of the stitch.

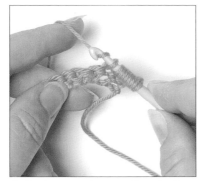

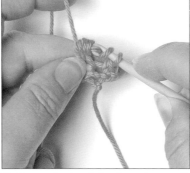

6. Again, wrap the yarn, from back to front, over the hook.

7. Draw the hook backward to pull the loop through all nine loops on the hook.

8. Continue to the end of the row, interpersing double crochet stitches with the bullion stitches.

HINTS
Bullions

If you slowly turn the hook as you pull it through all the loops it is less likely to become "stuck."

It is easier to create a neat bullion stitch with a fine hook and thread rather than a thick hook and thread.

To help even out the wraps, hold the stitch between your thumb and index finger and stroke the wraps with your thumb.

It is easier to work bullions with a slippery thread or yarn, such as rayon.

Clusters
Basic cluster with double crochet stitch

Here each cluster is made up of three double crochet stitches.

1. Stitch to the position for the cluster. Wrap the yarn, from back to front, over the hook.

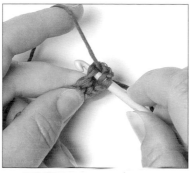

2. Take the hook, from front to back, through the top of the next stitch of the previous row.

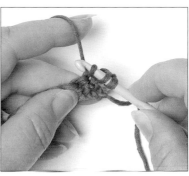

3. Again, wrap the yarn, from back to front, over the hook. Draw the hook backward to pull the yarn through the top of the stitch of the previous row. There are three loops on the hook.

4. Again, wrap the yarn, from back to front, over the hook. Draw the hook backward to pull the yarn through the first two loops on the hook. There are now two loops on the hook.

5. Wrap the yarn, from back to front, over the hook. Take the hook, from front to back, through the top of the next stitch of the previous row.

6. Again, wrap the yarn, from back to front, over the hook. Draw the hook backward to pull the yarn through the top of the stitch of the previous row. There are four loops on the hook.

Basic cluster with double crochet stitch / continued

7. Again, wrap the yarn, from back to front, over the hook. Draw the hook backward to pull the yarn through the first two loops on the hook. There are now three loops on the hook.

8. Repeat steps 5–7. You will have four loops on the hook.

9. Wrap the yarn, from back to front, over the hook. Draw the hook backward to pull the yarn through all the loops on the hook to complete the cluster.

10. Work two chain stitches.

11. Work a second cluster following steps 1–9.

12. Continue stitching clusters to the end of the row, working two chain stitches between each one.

HINTS
Clusters

Keep your tension fairly loose to maintain the softness of the cluster and make it easier to finish the final loop.

To maintain the same number of stitches in each row, work chain stitches between the clusters. The number of stitches in a cluster – 1 = the number of chain stitches required.

If you work shorter stitches between clusters, the clusters will stand out more.

Always make your turning chains match the height of any shorter stitches in a row, rather than match the height of the clusters.

Basic cluster with single crochet

Here each cluster is made up of three single crochet stitches.

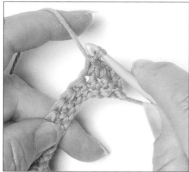

1. Stitch to the position for the cluster.

2. Take the hook, from front to back, through the top of the next stitch of the previous row.

3. Wrap the yarn, from back to front, over the hook.

4. Draw the hook backward to pull the yarn through the top of the stitch of the previous row. There are two loops on the hook.

5. Take the hook, from front to back, through the top of the next stitch of the previous row.

6. Wrap the yarn, from back to front, over the hook. Draw the hook backward to pull the yarn through the top of the stitch of the previous row. There are three loops on the hook.

7. Repeat steps 5–6. You will have four loops on the hook.

8. Wrap the yarn, from back to front, over the hook. Draw the hook backward to pull the yarn through all the loops on the hook to complete the cluster.

Basic cluster with single crochet / continued

9. Work two chain stitches.

10. Work a second cluster following steps 2–8.

11. Continue stitching clusters to the end of the row, working two chain stitches between each one.

Loop Stitches Basic loop stitch

Loop stitches can be spaced at intervals, worked in groups, or worked in every stitch in a row except for the edge stitches.

1. On a wrong-side row, work to the position for the loop (we have used single crochet).

2. Take the hook, from front to back, through the next stitch.

3. Wrap the yarn, from back to front, over the hook.

4. Catch the yarn on the other side of your index finger with the barb of the hook.

5. Draw the hook backward and pull both yarns through the stitch.

6. Wrap the yarn, from back to front, over the hook.

Loop stitches can be made in two ways: by working short lengths of chain stitches or by enlarging a stitch.

Stitches, stitches, stitches

Basic loop stitch / continued

7. Draw the hook backward and pull the yarn through all the loops on the hook. Drop the loop from your finger.

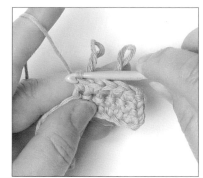

8. Work to the position for the next loop and repeat steps 2–7.

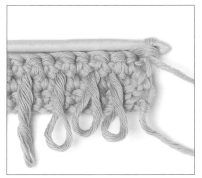

9. Continue almost to the end of the row, working loop stitches between your other stitches. Work the last one or two stitches as plain stitches.

Loop stitch worked over a frame

A pencil, ruler, strip of stiff cardboard, or something similar can be used for your frame.

1. On a wrong-side row, work one or two single crochet stitches.

2. Supporting the frame in your left hand, take the hook, from front to back, through the next stitch.

3. Transfer the frame to your right hand. Take the yarn, from front to back, around the frame.

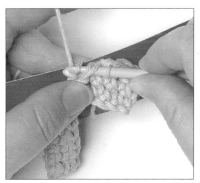

4. Transfer the frame back to your left hand. Wrap the yarn, from back to front, over the hook.

5. Draw the hook backward and pull the yarn through the stitch. There are two loops on the hook.

6. Wrap the yarn, from back to front, over the hook.

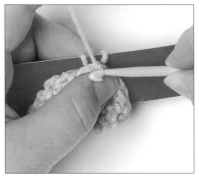

7. Draw the hook backward and pull the yarn through both loops on the hook.

8. Repeat steps 2–7 to work a second stitch in the same manner.

9. Continue working stitches in the same manner, slipping them off the other end of the frame if it becomes too full. Work single crochet for the last one or two stitches.

Basic loop stitch

Loop stitch worked over a frame

Fur stitch

Fur stitch

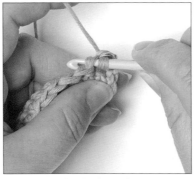

1. On a wrong-side row, work a single crochet.

2. Take the hook, from front to back, through the next stitch.

3. Keeping the hook to the right of the yarn, pick up the yarn on the far side of your left finger with the barb of the hook.

Fur stitch / continued

4. Raise your finger to the height you wish the loop to be.

5. Pull the yarn through the stitch, taking care not to catch the front of the loop. There are two loops on the hook.

6. Keeping the hook to the left of the loop, take the yarn, from back to front, over the hook.

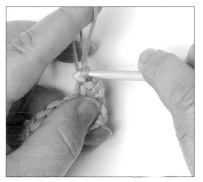

7. Draw the hook backward and pull the yarn through both loops on the hook.

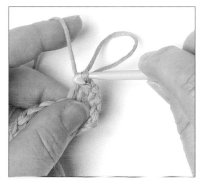

8. Drop the loop from your finger and pick up the working yarn again.

9. Repeat steps 2–8 to work a second stitch.

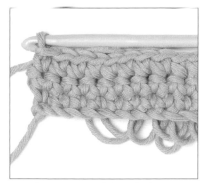

10. Continue working stitches across the row in the same manner. Work the last stitch as a single crochet.

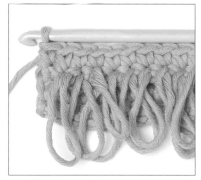

11. Work one chain, turn your work, and work a row of single crochet.

12. Continue alternating rows of fur stitch and single crochet until your work is the desired length.

Chain loop stitch

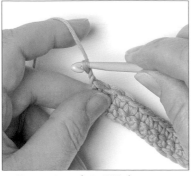

1. Rows 1 and 2. Work two rows of single crochet. Work one turning chain.

2. Row 3. Turn your work. Take your hook, from front to back, through the front loop of the next single crochet of the previous row.

3. Complete the single crochet stitch in the usual manner.

4. Work a single crochet into the next stitch, again taking the hook under the front loop of the stitch only. Work five chains.

5. Repeat step 4 along the row until reaching the last stitch.

6. Work a single crochet into the last stitch in the same manner as before. Work one turning chain.

7. Row 4. Turn your work. Take the hook, from front to back, through the remaining loop of the next stitch in row 2.

8. Complete the single crochet stitch in the usual manner.

9. Work a single crochet into the next stitch, again only taking the hook under the remaining loop of the next stitch in row 2.

Stitches, stitches, stitches

Chain loop stitch / continued

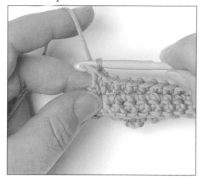

10. Repeat step 9 along the row until reaching the last stitch.

11. Work a single crochet into the last stitch in the same manner as before. Work one turning chain.

12. Subsequent rows. Repeat rows 3–4 until your fabric is the desired length.

Astrakhan stitch
Astrakhan stitch is worked back and forth across the fabric without turning it.

1. Row 1. Work a row of double crochet.

2. Row 2. (Work left to right.) Work five chains.

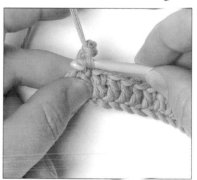

3. Take your hook, from front to back, into the front loop at the top of the second to last double crochet of the previous row.

4. Keeping the chains behind your hook, catch the yarn in the barb of the hook.

5. Pull the yarn through both the stitch and loop on the hook to form a slip stitch.

6. Repeat steps 2–4 along the row up to the last stitch, working a slip stitch into the front loop of the next double crochet each time.

7. Work five chains and then work a slip stitch, taking the hook through both loops of the third turning chain in the previous row.

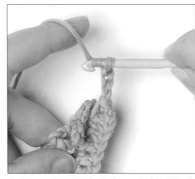

8. Row 3. (Work right to left.) Work three chains. Wrap the yarn, from back to front, over the hook.

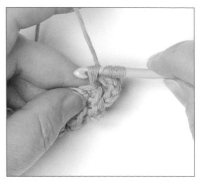

9. Take the hook, from front to back, through the back loop at the top of the first double crochet.

10. Complete a double crochet stitch.

11. Continue working a double crochet stitch into the back loop of each double crochet in the first row.

12. Subsequent rows. Repeat steps 2–7 to work the fourth row.

13. Repeat steps 8–11 to work a fifth row.

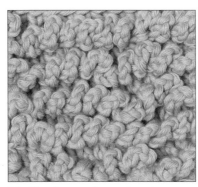

14. Continue, alternating between a row of loops worked from left to right and a row of double crochet worked from right to left, until your work is the desired length.

HINTS
Loop stitches

Work one or two plain stitches at the end of each row so it is easier to assemble your project.

Forming even loops takes a little practice so don't give up too quickly.

Vary the number of chains when working chain loop stitch and astrakhan stitch to achieve different looks.

Picots

1. On a right-side row, work to the position for the picot (we have used single crochet).

2. Work five chains.

3. Take the hook, from front to back, through the first chain.

4. Wrap the yarn, from back to front, over the hook.

5. Draw the hook backward and pull the loop through both the chain stitch and loop already on the hook to form a slip stitch. A picot is created.

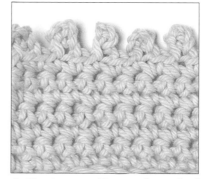

6. Work to the position for the next picot.

7. Work a second picot following steps 2–5.

8. Continue working to the end of the row, working the picots between your other stitches.

Popcorns

A popcorn is formed in the same way as a shell but the stitches are folded over at the top. Our popcorn is made with four double crochet stitches but you can use more.

1. On a right-side row, stitch to the position for the popcorn. Wrap the yarn, from back to front, over the hook.

2. Skip one stitch and then take the hook, from front to back, through the top of the next stitch of the previous row.

3. Complete the double crochet stitch (see pages 19–21).

4. Again, wrap the yarn, from back to front, over the hook. Take the hook through the top of the same stitch as before.

5. Work a second double crochet stitch.

6. Work two more double crochet stitches into the same stitch of the previous row.

Popcorns / continued

7. Remove the hook from the loop. Take the hook, from front to back, through the top of the first double crochet and then through the loop.

8. Draw the hook backward to pull the loop through the double crochet stitch.

9. Continue to the end of the row, interspersing popcorns with your selected stitches (we have used single crochet).

Puff Stitches

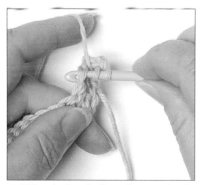

1. On a wrong-side row, work to the position for the puff stitch.

2. Wrap the yarn, from back to front, over the hook.

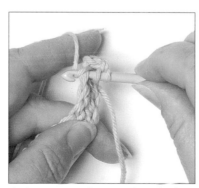

3. Take the hook, from front to back, through the top of the next stitch of the previous row.

4. Again, wrap the yarn, from back to front, over the hook.

5. Draw the hook backward to pull the loop through the top of the stitch. There are three loops on the hook.

Puff stitches are worked in a similar manner to bobbles but they use half double crochet stitch rather than double crochet stitch.

Stitches, stitches, stitches

51

6. Tilt the tip of the hook upward to lengthen the first loop on the hook.

7. Again, wrap the yarn, from back to front, over the hook.

8. Take the hook, from front to back, through the top of the same stitch as before.

9. Wrap the yarn, from back to front, over the hook. Draw the hook backward to pull the yarn through the top of the stitch of the previous row. There are five loops on the hook.

10. Again, tilt the tip of the hook upward to lengthen the first loop on the hook.

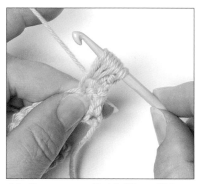

11. Repeat steps 7–10. You will have seven loops on the hook.

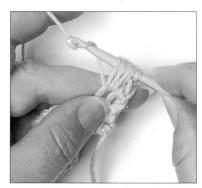

12. Wrap the yarn, from back to front, over the hook.

13. Draw the hook backward to pull the yarn through all the loops on the hook.

14. Wrap the yarn, from back to front, over the hook.

Stitches, stitches, stitches

15. Draw the hook backward to pull the yarn through the remaining loop on the hook and secure the puff stitch.

16. Continue stitching to the end of the row, working the puff stitches between your other stitches.

HINTS
Puff stitch

Like bobbles, these stitches look their best when worked in rows of shorter stitches.

As you stitch, place your index finger over the loops on the hook so you don't shorten them when working the next part of the puff stitch.

Raised Stitches Front-post double crochet

This method pushes the double crochet stitches forward and creates a raised horizontal line on the back.

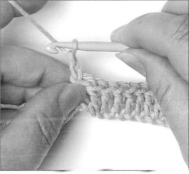

1. Work at least a row of dc before beginning the raised stitches.

2. Work two turning chains.

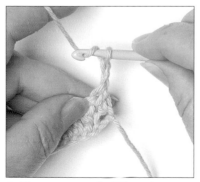

3. Turn your work. Wrap the yarn, from back to front, over the hook.

4. Take the hook, from right to left, behind the second stitch of the previous row.

5. Again, wrap the yarn, from back to front, over the hook.

Raised stitches add texture to your crocheted fabric. The following stitches create either horizontal or vertical ribs on your fabric.

Stitches, stitches, stitches

53

6. Draw the hook backward to pull the loop of yarn through. There are three loops on the hook.

7. Again, wrap the yarn, from back to front, over the hook. Draw the hook backward to pull the yarn through the first two loops on the hook. There are now two loops on the hook.

8. Again, wrap the yarn, from back to front, over the hook. Draw the hook backward to pull the yarn through the remaining two loops on the hook and complete the stitch.

9. Wrap the yarn, from back to front, over the hook. Work a second stitch, following steps 4–8.

10. Continue working stitches to the end of the row in the same manner.

Back-post double crochet

This method pushes the double crochet stitches away from you and creates a raised horizontal line on the front.

1. Work at least one row of double crochet before beginning the raised stitches.

2. Work two turning chains.

Back-post double crochet / continued

3. Turn your work. Wrap the yarn, from back to front, over the hook

4. Take the hook, from back to front, through the space between the first and second stitches of the previous row.

5. Take the hook, from front to back, through the space between the second and third stitches of the previous row.

6. Again, wrap the yarn, from back to front, over the hook.

7. Draw the hook backward to pull the loop of yarn through. There are three loops on the hook.

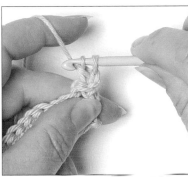

8. Again, wrap the yarn, from back to front, over the hook. Draw the hook backward to pull the yarn through the first two loops on the hook. There are now two loops on the hook.

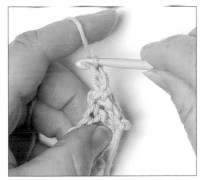

9. Again, wrap the yarn, from back to front, over the hook. Draw the hook backward to pull the yarn through the remaining two loops on the hook and complete the stitch.

10. Wrap the yarn, from back to front, over the hook. Work a second stitch, following steps 4–9 but taking the hook behind the third stitch of the previous row.

11. Continue working stitches to the end of the row in the same manner.

Stitches, stitches, stitches

Front-post and back-post double crochet rib

This method combines alternating front-post and back-post double crochet stitches.

1. Work at least one row of double crochet before beginning the raised stitches.

2. Work two turning chains.

3. Turn your work. Wrap the yarn, from back to front, over the hook.

4. Work a front-post double crochet following steps 4–8 on pages 53–54.

5. Wrap the yarn, from back to front, over the hook.

6. Take the hook, from back to front, through the space between the second and third stitches of the previous row.

7. Take the hook, from front to back, through the space between the third and fourth stitches of the previous row.

8. Again, wrap the yarn, from back to front, over the hook.

Front-post and back-post double crochet rib / continued

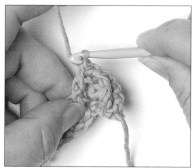

9. Complete the stitch by following steps 7–9 on page 55. This is a back-post double crochet stitch.

10. Wrap yarn, from back to front, over hook. Work an FPdc stitch in same manner as before but take the hook behind the stem of the next stitch of the previous row.

11. Wrap the yarn, from back to front, over the hook. Take the hook in front of the next stitch of the previous row and work a BPdc stitch.

12. Continue working stitches to the end of the row, alternating between a front-post and back-post double crochet.

13. Work two turning chains. Turn your work.

14. To maintain the vertical rib, begin with a back-post double crochet if the stitch of the previous row is pushed back. Begin with a front-post double crochet if the stitch of the previous row is pushed forward.

15. Continue working to the end of the row, alternating between back-post and front-post double crochet stitches.

HINTS
Raised stitches

Raised stitches are also known as post stitches and relief stitches.

Use only two turning chains for a row of front-post and back-post double crochet rather than the usual three chains. Because the hook is taken through the middle of a stitch in the previous row rather than the top, the rows are not as high as basic double crochet rows.

If you want the raised sections to always fall on the same side of the fabric, alternate between rows of front-post double crochet and back-post double crochet.

Stitches, stitches, stitches

Shells Basic shell

Here each shell is made up of three double crochet stitches.

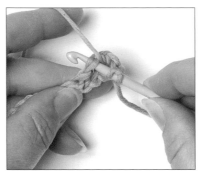

1. Work to the position for the shell. Wrap the yarn, from back to front, over the hook.

2. Skip one stitch and then take the hook, from front to back, through the top of the next stitch of the previous row.

3. Complete the double crochet stitch (see pages 19–21).

4. Again, wrap the yarn, from back to front, over the hook. Take the hook through the top of the same stitch as before.

5. Wrap the yarn, from back to front, over the hook and complete the double crochet stitch.

6. Work a third double crochet stitch into exactly the same stitch of the previous row to complete the first shell.

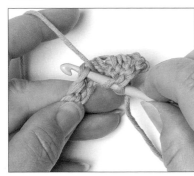

7. Wrap the yarn, from back to front, over the hook. Skip two stitches and then take the hook, from front to back, through the top of the next stitch of the previous row.

8. Work three double crochet stitches into this stitch to form a second shell.

9. Continue working shells to the end of the row, leaving two stitches of the previous row between the base of each shell.

Fan stitch
This is an extension of the shell stitch. It uses many more double crochet stitches.

Basic shell

1. Work a foundation chain that is a multiple of 14 plus 2.

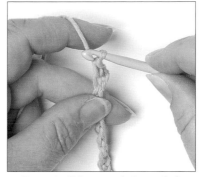

2. **Row 1.** Skip one chain and then work a single crochet into the next chain.

HINTS
Shells

When making long stitches, keep the tip of a finger on the long loop to prevent it from being pulled and shortened.

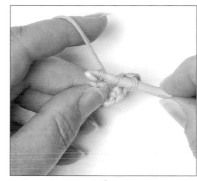

3. Wrap the yarn, from back to front, over the hook. Skip six chains and take the hook through the next chain.

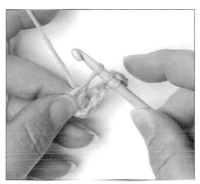

4. Wrap the yarn as before and pull through the chain, pulling through a loop approximately ⅝" (15 mm) long.

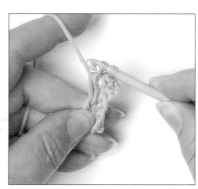

5. Wrap the yarn as before and draw the hook backward to pull the yarn through the first two loops on the hook.

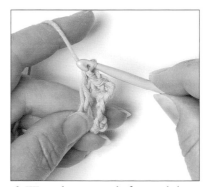

6. Wrap the yarn as before and draw the hook backward to pull the yarn through the remaining two loops on the hook.

Stitches, stitches, stitches

59

Fan stitch / continued

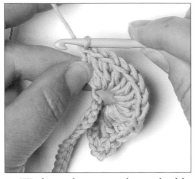

7. Work twelve more long double crochet stitches into the same chain as the first double crochet stitch.

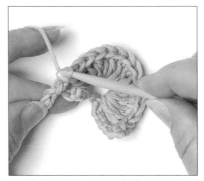

8. Skip six chains and then work a single crochet.

9. Repeat steps 3–8 to the end of the foundation chain.

10. Work three turning chains.

11. Row 2. Turn your work. Work a long double crochet stitch into the first single crochet.

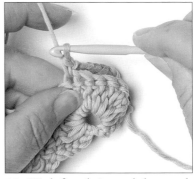

12. Work five chains and then work a single crochet into the seventh double crochet of the fan.

13. Work five chains and then work two long double crochet stitches into the top of the single crochet between the two fans.

14. Repeat steps 12–13 to the end of the row. Finish with two long double crochet stitches into the last single crochet.

15. Work one turning chain.

16. Row 3. Turn your work and work a single crochet between the first pair of long double crochet stitches of the previous row.

17. Work thirteen long double crochet stitches into the single crochet at the middle of the first fan in the previous row.

18. Work a single crochet between the next pair of long double crochet stitches of the previous row.

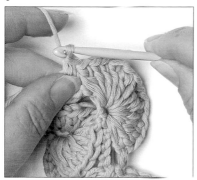

19. Repeat steps 17–18 to the end of the row.

20. Work three turning chains.

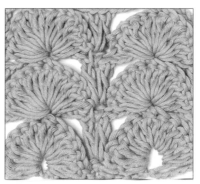

21. Subsequent rows. Repeat rows 2 and 3 until your fabric is the desired length.

Spike Stitches

These stitches are worked over the top of other stitches. They can be worked in groups or on their own.

1. On a right-side row, work to the position for the spike (we have used single crochet).

2. Take the hook, from front to back, through the next stitch in an earlier row.

3. Wrap the yarn, from back to front, over the hook.

4. Draw the hook backward to pull the loop through the stitch.

5. Pull the loop through until it comes to the same height as the previous stitches of the row.

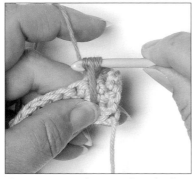

6. Again, wrap the yarn, from back to front, over the hook.

7. Draw the hook backward to pull the yarn through the two loops on the hook.

8. Work to the position of the next spike.

9. Work a second spike following steps 2–7.

10. Continue stitching to the end of the row, working the spikes between your other stitches.

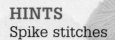

HINTS
Spike stitches

Spikes can be worked in groups or individually.

Spikes are particularly effective when you use more than one color of yarn.

Crocheting with Beads and Sequins

Threading beads and sequins

Beads and sequins need to be threaded onto your yarn before you begin and there are several methods you can use. Choose the method that suits you and your materials the best.

If your beads need to appear on your garment in a certain sequence, thread them in reverse. The last bead you thread will be the first bead you crochet into your work. Thread cup-shaped sequins so the inside of the cup faces away from the ball of yarn.

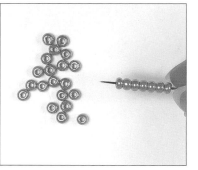

1. Thread the end of the yarn into a sewing needle and simply scoop up the beads with the tip of the needle. However, if you cannot pass the needle and yarn through the beads, try one of the following:

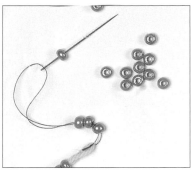

2. Thread a doubled length of sewing thread into a needle. Pass the end of the yarn through the loop of the thread. Scoop up the beads with the needle and then push them along the sewing thread and onto the yarn.

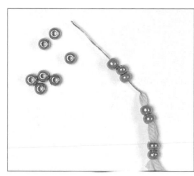

3. Place the end of the yarn over a piece of fuse wire approximately 2" (5 cm) long. Fold the wire over the yarn and twist the two halves of wire together. Thread the beads onto the fuse wire and down onto the yarn.

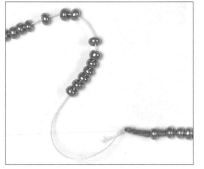

4. Purchase beads that are already strung. Tie the end of the yarn to the end of the bead string and slide the beads onto the yarn.

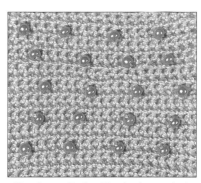

Beads applied with single crochet

Beads applied with double crochet

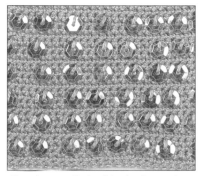

Sequins applied with single crochet

Applying beads with single crochet

1. Thread the beads onto the yarn. On a wrong-side row, stitch to the position for the bead. Slide a bead along the yarn until it rests against the right side of your work.

2. Holding the bead in place, take the hook, from front to back, through the top of the next stitch of the previous row.

3. Wrap the yarn, from back to front, over the hook.

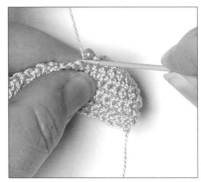

4. Pull the loop of yarn through the stitch. There are two loops on the hook.

5. Again, wrap the yarn, from back to front, over the hook. Pull the yarn through the loops on the hook to complete the stitch.

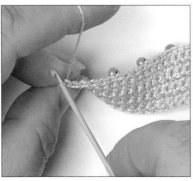

6. Continue adding beads across the row in the same manner, positioning them at the desired intervals.

More stitches and techniques

Applying beads with double crochet

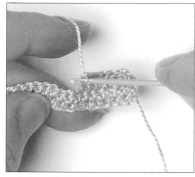

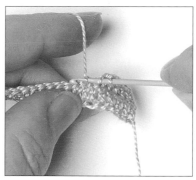

1. Thread the beads onto the yarn. On a wrong-side row, work to the position for the bead.

2. Wrap the yarn, from back to front, over the hook. Take the hook, from front to back, through the top of the next stitch of the previous row.

3. Again, wrap the yarn, from back to front, over the hook and pull it through the stitch of the previous row. There are three loops on the hook.

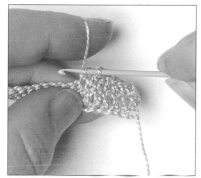

4. Again, wrap the yarn, from back to front, over the hook and pull it through two loops on the hook. There are now two loops on the hook.

5. Slide a bead along the yarn until it rests against the right side of your work.

6. Holding the bead in place, wrap the yarn, from back to front, over the hook on the other side of the bead.

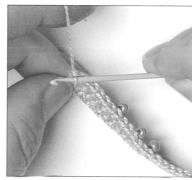

7. Pull the loop of yarn through the two loops on the hook to anchor the bead and complete the stitch.

8. Continue adding beads across the row in the same manner, positioning them at the desired intervals.

More stitches and techniques

Applying sequins This method will work with any of the basic stitches.

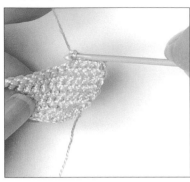

1. Thread the sequins onto the yarn. On a wrong-side row, work to the position for the sequin.

2. Work the stitch until the last two loops remain on the hook.

3. Slide a sequin along the yarn until it rests against the right side of your work.

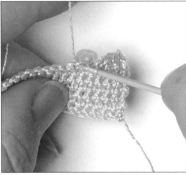

4. Holding the sequin in place, wrap the yarn, from back to front, over the hook on the other side of the sequin.

5. Pull the yarn through the loops on the hook to complete the stitch.

6. Continue adding sequins across the row in the same manner, positioning them at the desired intervals.

Broomstick Crochet

Like afghan crochet, a row of broomstick crochet is worked in two parts: a picking-up row and a fastening off row. The "broomstick" is usually a very large knitting needle.

The length of your broomstick determines the width of your crocheted piece.

For our example, we have used a multiple of five, but multiples of other numbers will work equally as well.

1. Work a foundation chain the required length. Make sure it is a multiple of five plus one.

2. Work single crochet across the foundation chain, following the instructions on pages 15–16.

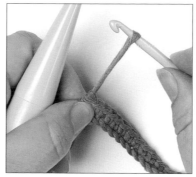

3. First row of loops: picking up. Hold the broomstick in your left hand and enlarge the loop on your hook.

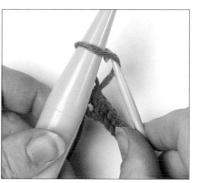

4. Slip the loop onto the broomstick.

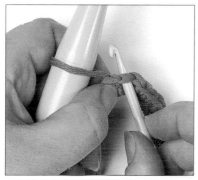

5. Take the hook through the next stitch.

6. Wrap the yarn, from front to back, around the hook.

7. Draw the hook backward to form a new loop on the hook.

8. Enlarge the loop as before and slip it onto the broomstick.

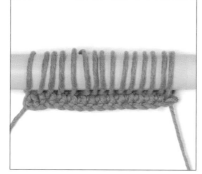

9. Repeat steps 5–8 until the entire row is worked.

10. First row of loops: fastening off. Carefully slip the first five loops off the broomstick. Take your hook, from right to left, through the loops.

More stitches and techniques

Broomstick crochet / continued

11. Wrap the yarn, from back to front, around the hook.

12. Draw the hook backward to pull a loop of yarn through the five large loops.

13. Work a single chain stitch.

14. Taking the hook through the five large loops each time, work five single crochet into the group of loops.

15. Slip the next five loops off the broomstick and onto the hook.

16. Work a single chain stitch and then five single crochet stitches into the group of loops.

17. Repeat steps 15–16 to the end of the row.

18. Second row of loops: picking up. Again, pick up the broomstick with your left hand. Enlarge the loop on the hook and slip it onto the broomstick.

More stitches and techniques

Broomstick crochet / continued

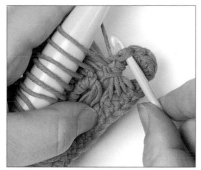

19. Pick up a loop through the top of each single crochet in the previous row and place it on the broomstick.

20. Second row of loops: fastening off. Fasten off in exactly the same manner as the first row of loops.

21. Subsequent rows. Work remaining rows in the same manner as the second row. Trim yarn and fasten off following the instructions on page 24.

Chevrons Increases and decreases are used to create a zigzag effect.

Basic chevron This method works for all the basic stitches, but you will need to adjust the number of turning chains in your foundation chain.

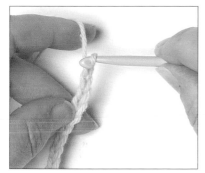

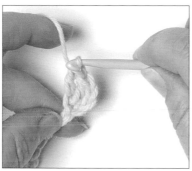

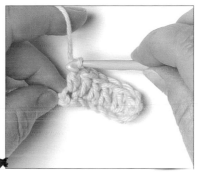

1. Work the foundation chain, making sure it is a multiple of eleven stitches plus four.

2. Row 1. Skip three chains (the turning chains) and work two double crochet stitches into the next chain.

3. Work a double crochet into each of the next four chains.

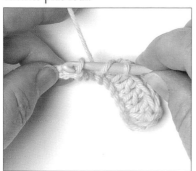

4. Wrap the yarn over the hook, skip two chains, and take the hook through the next chain.

5. Complete a double crochet and then work a double crochet into each of the next three chains.

6. Work three double crochet stitches into the next chain.

More stitches and techniques

7. Repeat steps 3–6 across the row, ending with two double crochet stitches into the last chain.

8. Work three turning chains and turn your work.

9. Row 2. Work two double crochet stitches into the first double crochet of the previous row.

✷ **10.** Work a double crochet into each of the next four double crochet stitches of the previous row.

11. Skip two double crochet stitches of the previous row and then work a double crochet into each of the next four double crochet stitches of the previous row.

12. Work three double crochet stitches into the next double crochet of the previous row. ✣

13. Repeat steps 10–12 across the row, ending with two double crochet stitches into the top of the turning chain of the previous row.

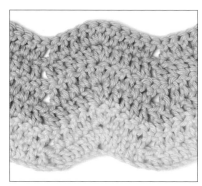

14. Work all subsequent rows in the same manner as row 2.

HINTS
Working chevrons

When working chevron stripes, carry the yarn up the side of the work in the same manner as for basic stripes (see page 101).

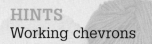

More stitches and techniques

70

Wavy chevron

This method works for all the basic stitches, but you will need to adjust the number of turning chains in your foundation chain.

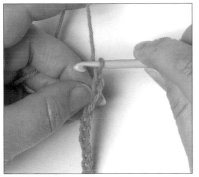

1. Work the foundation chain, making sure it is a multiple of fourteen stitches plus three.

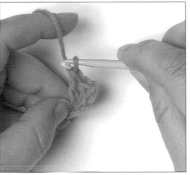

2. Row 1. Skip three chains (the turning chain) and work two double crochet stitches into the next chain.

3. Work a double crochet into each of the next three chains.

4. Over the next three chains, work three double crochet stitches together (see page 33).

5. Repeat step 4.

6. Work a double crochet into each of the next three chains.

7. Work three double crochet stitches into the next chain.

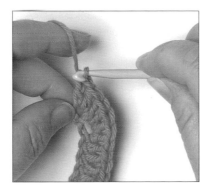

8. Repeat step 7.

9. Repeat steps 3–8 across the row, finishing with three double crochet stitches into the last chain.

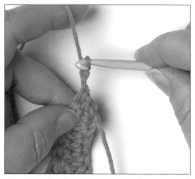

10. Work three turning chains and turn your work.

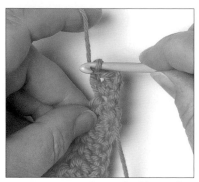

11. Row 2. Work two double crochet stitches into the top of the first double crochet of the previous row.

12. Work a double crochet into each of the next three double crochet stitches of the previous row.

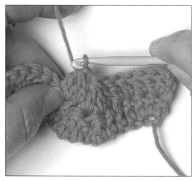

13. Over the next three double crochet stitches of the previous row, work three double crochet stitches together (see page 33). Repeat once.

14. Work a double crochet into each of the next three double crochet stitches of the previous row.

15. Work three double crochet stitches into the top of the next double crochet of the previous row. Repeat once.

16. Repeat steps 12–15 across the row, ending with three double crochet stitches into the top turning chain of the previous row.

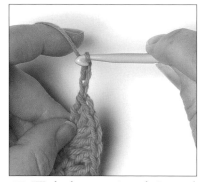

17. Work three turning chains and turn your work.

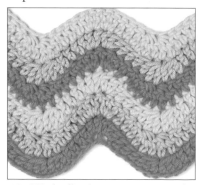

18. Work all subsequent rows in the same manner as row 2.

More stitches and techniques

Circular Crochet
In circular crochet, you don't need to turn your work after each round. A variety of shapes can all be made using the techniques of circular crochet.

Motifs

Circle
Evenly space the increases within each round.

Triangle
Make the increases at three evenly spaced positions in a round. Position the increases at the same place in each round.

Square
Make the increases at four evenly spaced positions in a round. Position the increases at the same place in each round.

Pentagon
Make the increases at five evenly spaced positions in a round. Position the increases at the same place in each round.

Hexagon
Make the increases at six evenly spaced positions in a round. Position the increases at the same place in each round.

Octagon
Make the increases at eight evenly spaced positions in a round. Position the increases at the same place in each round.

HINTS Circular crochet

If working a patchwork project, leave the tails of yarn long enough to sew the motifs together.

The taller the stitch you use in a round, the more increases you will need within the round to keep the motif flat.

More stitches and techniques

73

More stitches and techniques

1. Foundation. Make a slipknot using method 1 on page 12 and place it on the hook. Work several chain stitches (your pattern will specify how many are required).

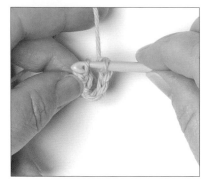

2. Take the hook, from front to back, through the middle of the first chain.

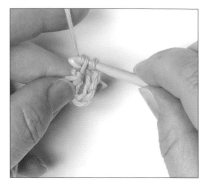

3. Wrap the yarn, from back to front, over the hook.

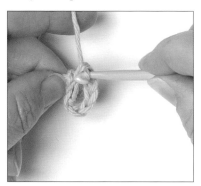

4. Draw your hook backward to pull the loop through both loops on the hook, forming a slip stitch.

5. Gently pull the dangling tail of yarn to tighten the first stitch.

6. Row 1. Work the required number of turning chains for your stitch (we have worked three chains since our sample uses double crochet stitch).

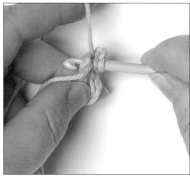

7. Wrap the yarn around the hook and take the hook, from front to back, through the circle of foundation chains.

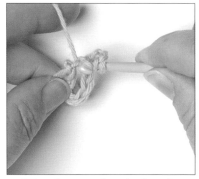

8. Wrap the yarn, from back to front, over the hook. Pull the loop of yarn through the circle.

9. Complete the double crochet stitch.

10. Continue working the desired number of stitches around the circle, taking the hook through the circle each time.

11. After working the last stitch, work a slip stitch into the top turning chain to complete the round.

Beginning a circular motif: method 2

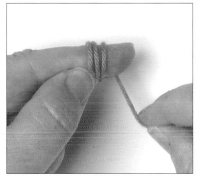

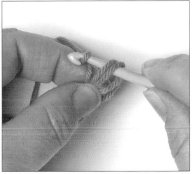

1. Foundation. Hold the end of the yarn between the thumb and index finger of your left hand.

2. Wrap the yarn clockwise around the tip of your finger several times. Make sure the end is held in place.

3. Carefully slip the yarn ring from your finger and onto the hook. Wrap yarn, from back to front, over hook.

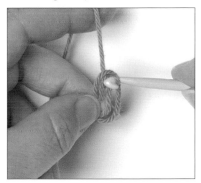

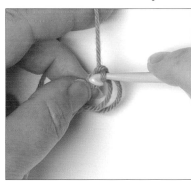

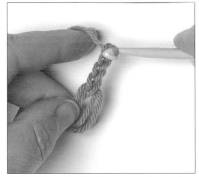

4. Pull the wrap through the yarn ring, taking care to pull through the wrapped section of yarn only.

5. Work a chain stitch to secure the ring.

6. Row 1. Work the required number of turning chains for your stitch (we have worked three chains since our sample uses double crochet stitch).

More stitches and techniques

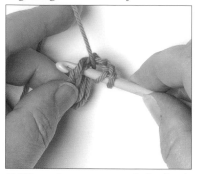

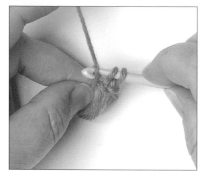

7. Wrap the yarn around the hook and take the hook, from front to back, through the yarn ring.

8. Wrap the yarn, from back to front, over the hook. Pull the loop of yarn through the yarn ring.

9. Following steps 9–11 on pages 74–75, complete the round of stitches.

Working a circular motif

1. Foundation and row 1. Complete the first round following the instructions on pages 74–75 or pages 75–76.

2. Work the required number of turning chains for your stitch (we have worked three chains because our sample uses double crochet stitch).

3. Work the round, following your pattern and working the required number of increases for your shape (your pattern will specify these).

Fastening off the final round: method 1

4. Repeat steps 2–3 until your motif is complete.

1. After working the last stitch, work a slip stitch into the top of the turning chain of the previous row.

2. Cut the yarn, leaving a tail. Catch the tail with the hook.

3. Draw the hook backward to pull the yarn through the loop on the hook. Continue pulling until the yarn is completely through.

4. Hold the last chain stitch firmly and tug on the tail of yarn to tighten.

5. Weave in the tail of yarn following the instructions on pages 24–25.

Fastening off the final round: method 2

1. After completing the last stitch, cut the yarn, leaving a tail. Catch the tail with the hook.

2. Draw the hook backward to pull the yarn through the loop on the hook. Continue pulling until the yarn is completely through.

3. Hold the last chain stitch firmly and tug on the tail of yarn to tighten.

4. Thread the tail into a tapestry needle. With the right side of the work facing you, take the needle, from front to back, under both loops of the stitch next to the turning chain.

5. Pull the yarn through. Take the needle through the center of the last stitch of the round.

6. Pull the yarn through until the stitch looks the same as the other stitches. Weave in the tail of yarn following the instructions on pages 24–25.

More stitches and techniques

Entrelac Crochet

Like *entrelac* knitting, *entrelac* crochet is reminiscent of patchwork and is very effective when worked with multiple colors. It is made up of a series of diamond shapes.

Base row of diamonds

1. Determine the width you require by using the following formula: No. of diamonds x no. of stitches across one diamond, plus one.

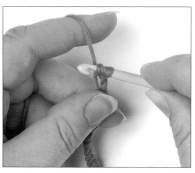

2. First diamond. Take hook through second chain. Wrap yarn, from back to front, and draw the yarn through the chain to form a loop on the hook.

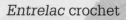

Entrelac crochet

In this example, we have worked 3 diamonds, each 10 stitches wide: 3 x 10 = 30.

Work a foundation chain with this number of stitches plus 1.

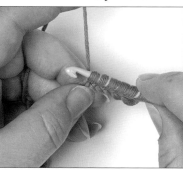

3. Repeat the procedure in the next five chains. You will have seven loops on your hook.

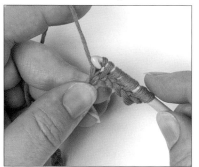

4. Wrap the yarn, from back to front, over the hook. Draw the hook backward to pull the new wrap through the first loop on the hook.

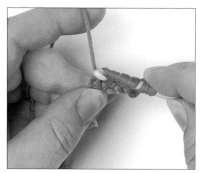

5. Again, wrap yarn, from back to front, over hook. Draw hook backward to pull the new wrap through the first two loops on the hook.

6. Repeat step 5 until only one loop remains on the hook.

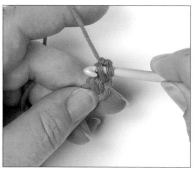

7. Take the hook, from right to left, behind the second vertical bar of the previous row.

8. Wrap the yarn, from back to front, over hook. Draw hook backward to pull the wrap behind the vertical bar. There are two loops on the hook.

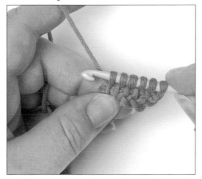

9. Pick up a loop through each vertical bar of the previous row in the same manner. You will have six loops on your hook.

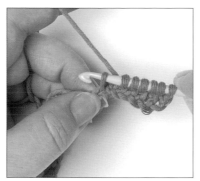

10. Take your hook through the next chain.

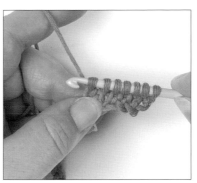

11. Wrap the yarn and pick up a loop in the same manner as before.

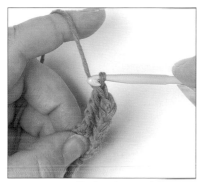

12. Fasten off the loops following steps 4–6.

13. Work three more rows in the same manner, picking up a new chain at the end of each picking-up row.

14. Take your hook behind the second vertical bar of the previous row.

15. Wrap the yarn and pull through both the vertical bar and loop on the hook to form a slip stitch.

16. Repeat through each vertical bar.

17. Take the hook through the last chain you used in the previous row.

More stitches and techniques

. . . .

79

18. Work a slip stitch as before.

19. Second diamond. Take the hook through the next chain. Wrap the yarn, from back to front, and draw the yarn through the chain to form a loop on the hook.

20. Repeat the procedure in the next five chains. You will have seven loops on your hook.

21. Complete this diamond in the same manner as the first diamond.

22. Subsequent diamonds. Work all remaining diamonds in the same manner.

23. Trim the yarn, leaving a 6" (15 cm) tail. Pull the tail through the loop on the hook and fasten off the yarn.

Second row of diamonds

1. First diamond. Take your hook, from front to back, through the first slip stitch on the first diamond of the base row.

2. Wrap a new yarn, from front to back, over the hook and pull the yarn through to form a loop on the hook.

3. Pick up a loop through the next five slip stitches in the same manner.

More stitches and techniques

4. Pick up a loop through the first end stitch of the second diamond. You will have seven loops on your hook.

5. Fasten off the stitches following steps 4–6 on page 78.

6. Following steps 7–9 on pages 78–79, pick up a new loop through every vertical bar of the previous row. You will have six loops on your hook.

7. Take your hook through the next end stitch of the second base diamond.

8. Wrap the yarn as before and pull the new loop through.

9. Fasten off the stitches as before and work three more rows in the same manner.

10. Work a slip stitch through each vertical bar in the previous row as you did in the base row of diamonds.

11. Take the hook through the last stitch in the previous row.

More stitches and techniques

81

12. Work a slip stitch as before.

13. Second diamond. Pick up a loop through every slip stitch of the second diamond of the base row. You will have seven loops on the hook.

14. Work this diamond and all subsequent diamonds across the row in the same manner as the previous diamond.

Third row of diamonds

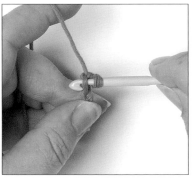

1. First diamond. Using a new yarn, work a foundation chain of six stitches. Take the hook through the second chain.

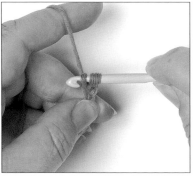

2. Wrap the yarn, from back to front, and draw the yarn through the chain to form a loop on the hook.

3. Repeat the procedure in the next four chains. You will have six loops on your hook.

4. Pick up a loop through the first end stitch of the first diamond in the second row. You will now have seven loops on your hook.

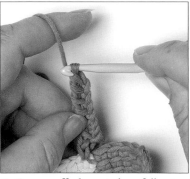

5. Fasten off the stitches following steps 4–6 on page 78.

6. Complete the diamond in the same manner as those in the second row of diamonds.

More stitches and techniques

82

Third row of diamonds / continued

7. Work all diamonds except for the last one in the same manner as the second row of diamonds.

8. Last diamond. Pick up a loop through each slip stitch of the last diamond in row 2. You will have six loops on your hook.

9. Pick up a seventh loop through the first slip stitch of the last diamond in row 1.

10. Fasten off the stitches in the same manner as for the previous diamonds.

11. Following steps 7–9 on pages 78–79, pick up a new loop through every vertical bar of the previous row. You will have six loops on your hook.

12. Take the hook through the side of the last stitch in the previous row and form a seventh loop.

13. Fasten off the stitches as before.

14. Repeat steps 11–13 three more times.

15. Work slip stitch across the previous stitches in the same manner as before to complete the diamond and row. Fasten off the yarn as before.

Subsequent rows of diamonds

Work the fourth row in exactly the same manner as the second row of diamonds. Continue working the required number of rows, alternating between the third and second rows.

> **HINTS** *Entrelac* crochet
>
> When fastening off with slip stitch at the end of a diamond, keep your stitches fairly loose. You will need to pick up your stitches for the next row of diamonds through these stitches.

Filet Crochet

Filet crochet features a square mesh background, and the design is created by filling in specific squares.

Chain and double crochet are the only stitches required to create this distinctive form of crochet. Individual double crochet stitches create the vertical bars of the mesh and pairs of double crochet stitches are used to fill in spaces or create blocks. Pairs of chain stitches create the horizontal bars of the mesh.

Patterns are often given in chart form, where each square on the chart represents either a space or a block.

Filet crochet is usually worked with mercerized cotton to give it a crisp, neat appearance. Fuzzy yarns tend to make the designs less distinct.

Working an open mesh

1. Work the desired number of foundation chains (this will be a multiple of three; see hints on page 92) and five chains.

2. First row. Wrap the yarn, from back to front, over the hook. Take the hook through the eighth chain from the hook.

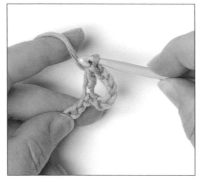

3. Complete the double crochet stitch to create a vertical bar.

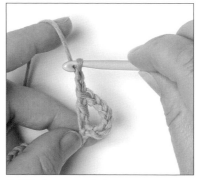

4. Work two chains to create a horizontal bar.

5. Wrap the yarn, from back to front, over the hook. Skip two foundation chains and take the hook through the next foundation chain.

6. Complete the double crochet stitch.

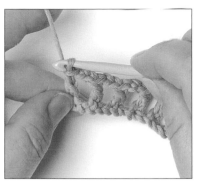

7. Repeat steps 4–6 to the end of the foundation chains.

8. Work five chains. This is really three turning chains and then a pair of chains for the first horizontal bar.

9. Second row. Turn your work. Wrap the yarn, from back to front, over the hook.

10. Take the hook, from front to back, through the top of the next double crochet stitch of the previous row.

11. Complete the double crochet stitch.

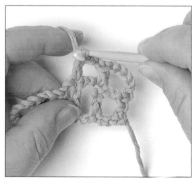

12. Work two chains and then a double crochet stitch into the top of the next double crochet stitch of the previous row.

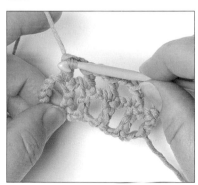

13. Repeat step 12 almost to the end of the row.

More stitches and techniques

85

Working an open mesh / continued

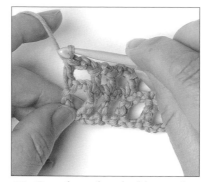

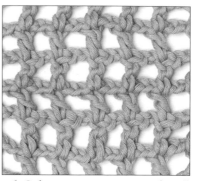

14. After working the last pair of chains, wrap yarn over hook and take hook through top turning chain of previous row. This is the third chain from the last double crochet stitch.

15. Complete the double crochet stitch.

16. Subsequent rows. Work all subsequent rows in the same manner as the second row, working five chains before turning.

Working filled blocks: checkerboard stitch

In our example we begin the first row with a block but you can also begin with a space. To do this, work the first square of the mesh following steps 1–3 on page 84.

1. Work the desired number of foundation chains (this will be a multiple of three; see hints on page 92) and three chains.

2. First row. Wrap the yarn, from back to front, over the hook. Take the hook through the fourth chain from the hook.

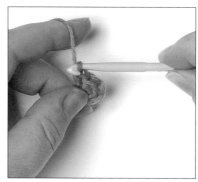

3. Complete the double crochet stitch.

4. Work a second double crochet into the next foundation chain to complete the block.

5. Work a double crochet into the next foundation chain to form a vertical bar.

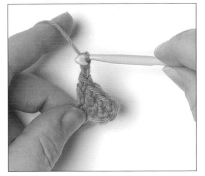

6. Work two chains to create a horizontal bar.

7. Wrap the yarn, from back to front, over the hook. Skip two foundation chains and take the hook through the next foundation chain.

8. Complete the double crochet stitch to form a vertical bar.

9. Work three more double crochet stitches: two for the block and one for the next vertical bar.

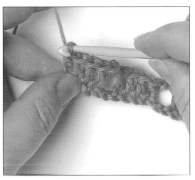

10. Repeat steps 6–9 to the end of the foundation chains. Depending on the number of stitches you have, you will finish with either one or four double crochet stitches.

11. If the row finished with one double crochet, work three turning chains. If the row finished with four double crochet stitches, work five chains: three turning chains and then a pair of chains for the horizontal bar.

12. Second row: beginning with a space. Turn your work. Wrap the yarn, from back to front, over the hook.

13. Take the hook, from front to back, through the top of the last vertical bar of the block in the previous row.

14. Complete the dc stitch.
Note: If your second row begins with a block, work steps 22–24 as the second row and steps 12–21 as the third row.

More stitches and techniques

87

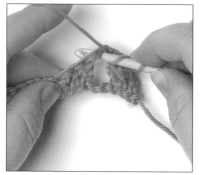

15. Wrap the yarn and take the hook, from front to back, through the space below the pair of chains.

16. Complete the double crochet stitch.

17. Wrap the yarn, from back to front, over the hook. Again, take the hook through the space of the previous row.

18. Complete the double crochet stitch.

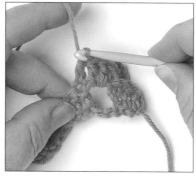

19. Work a fourth double crochet stitch into the top of the next vertical bar of the previous row.

20. Work two chains. Continue across the row, repeating skip two stitches, four dc and two chains. Finish with a dc into the top of the turning chain of the previous row.

21. Work three turning chains.

22. Third row: beginning with a block. Turn your work. Wrap the yarn, from back to front, over the hook.

23. Work two dc stitches into the space of the previous row, then a dc for the vertical bar. Continue across the row, repeating two chains, skip two stitches, and four dc stitches.

24. Work five chains: three turning chains and then a pair of chains for the horizontal bar.

25. Subsequent rows. Repeat the second row if you have an even number of blocks and spaces. Alternate between rows 2 and 3 if you have an uneven number of blocks and spaces.

Shaping filet crochet generally requires increasing and decreasing by blocks and spaces rather than stitches. This creates a stepped appearance to the edge.

Increasing a space at the end of a row

1. Work to the end of the row. Work two chains.

2. Wrap the yarn around the hook three times to begin a double triple crochet.

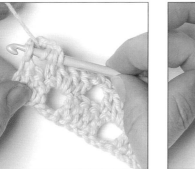

3. Take the hook, from front to back, through the same stitch as the last worked double crochet.

4. Complete the double triple crochet stitch.

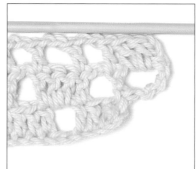

5. Work the required number of turning chains. Turn your work and continue across the row, following your pattern.

Increasing a space at the beginning of a row

1. Complete the required number of rows before the increase row. Work seven chains.

2. Turn your work. Work your first double crochet stitch into the last double crochet stitch of the previous row.

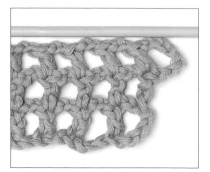

3. Continue across the row, following your pattern.

Increasing a block at the end of a row

1. Work to the end of the row. Work a triple crochet into the same stitch as the last double crochet.

2. Wrap the yarn around the hook twice to begin a second triple crochet. Take the hook behind the lowest crossover strand of the previous triple crochet.

3. Complete the triple crochet stitch.

4. Wrap the yarn around the hook once to begin a double crochet. Take the hook behind the lowest crossover strand of the previous triple crochet.

5. Complete the double crochet stitch.

6. Work the required number of turning chains. Turn your work and continue across the row, following your pattern.

Increasing a block at the beginning of a row

1. Complete the required number of rows before the increase row. Work five chains.

2. Turn your work. Work your first double crochet stitch into the fourth chain from the hook.

3. Work your second double crochet into the next chain and your third double crochet into the last double crochet of the previous row.

Decreasing a space at the beginning of a row

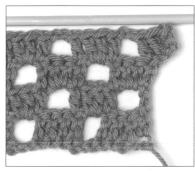

4. Continue across the row, following your pattern.

1. Complete the required number of rows before the decrease row. Work one chain.

2. Turn your work. Work a slip stitch into the top of the first chain of the horizontal bar of the previous row.

3. Work two more slip stitches, one into the second chain of the horizontal bar and one into the top of the next double crochet (this is a vertical bar).

4. Work your turning chains.

5. Continue across the row, following your pattern.

Decreasing a block at the beginning of a row

1. Complete the required number of rows before the decrease row. Work one chain.

2. Turn your work. Work a slip stitch into the top of the second double crochet (this is the last filling dc of the previous row, not the vertical bar).

3. Work two more slip stitches, one into each of the next two double crochet stitches.

4. Work your turning chains.

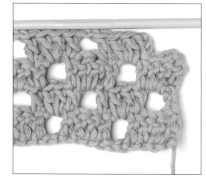

5. Continue across the row, following your pattern.

HINTS
Filet crochet
Charts generally do not show the foundation row of chains. To determine the number of foundation chains required, use the following formula: number of squares across the charted design x 3. To this, add 3 if you will be starting with a block or add 5 if you will be starting with a space. This allows for turning chains.

Decreasing at the end of a row

1. Work up to the point where you wish to finish the row, making sure you finish with a double crochet as a vertical bar.

2. Work your turning chains and turn your work.

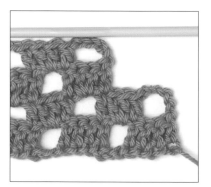

3. Continue across the row, following your pattern.

More stitches and techniques

Hairpin Crochet

Hairpin crochet is also known as hairpin lace or hairpin braid. You use both an ordinary crochet hook and a special hairpin loom to work it.

1. Hold the loom in your left hand between your thumb and index finger. Ensure the prongs face upward and the base rests in the palm of your hand.

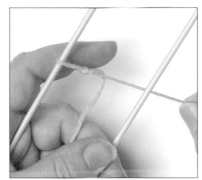

2. Make a slipknot and place it onto the left-hand pin of the hairpin loom.

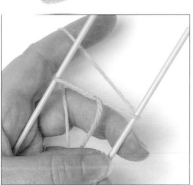

3. Holding the yarn as for regular crocheting, center the knot between the two prongs.

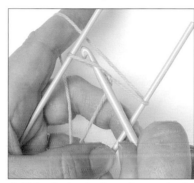

4. Take the hook, from front to back, through the loop on the left-hand prong.

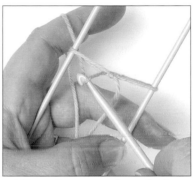

5. Wrap the yarn, from back to front, over the hook. Draw the hook backward to pull the wrap through the loop of yarn.

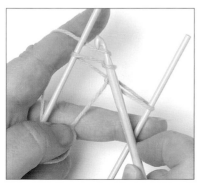

6. Again, wrap the yarn, from back to front, over the hook.

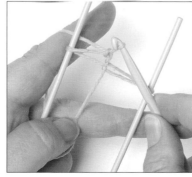

7. Draw the hook backward to pull the wrap through the loop on the hook.

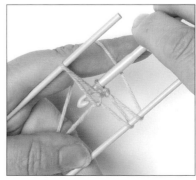

8. Holding the hook vertically, turn the loom 180° in a clockwise direction (the front is now at the back).

Hairpin crochet / continued

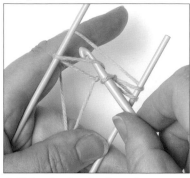

9. Take the hook, from bottom to top, behind the front of the loop around the left prong.

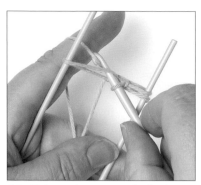

10. Pick up the yarn at the back.

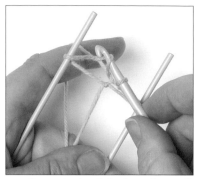

11. Draw the hook backward to pull the wrap through the loop of yarn around the left prong.

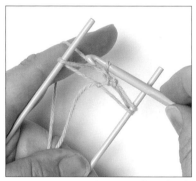

12. Again, wrap the yarn, from back to front, over the hook. Pull the wrap through both loops on the hook.

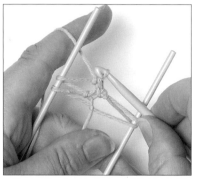

13. Repeat steps 8–12 to form a second stitch.

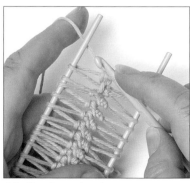

14. Continue in the same manner for the desired length.

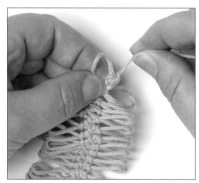

15. Remove the crochet from the loom and secure the yarn following the instructions on page 24.

HINTS
Hairpin crochet

Adjustable hairpin looms allow you to alter the width of your crochet. Some looms also have removable sections at both ends. These make it possible to work very long lengths because you can remove the base and let your earlier stitches drop off.

If you wish, you can finish the looped edges with a row of traditional crochet. Take care to keep all the loops twisted in the same direction.

When not crocheting, place the end plate onto the prongs to prevent your stitches from falling off.

More stitches and techniques

Irish Crochet

Irish crochet lace is made from separate stylized motifs, which are then set in a mesh background. It is worked with fine cotton or linen threads, and the motifs generally incorporate two threads: the working thread used to work the stitches and another thread or cord, known as a foundation cord or padding, over which the stitches are worked.

Working over a foundation cord: circle

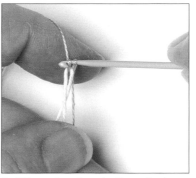

1. Make a slipknot with the working thread and place it on the hook. Fold a length of coarse thread in half. Take the hook, from front to back, through the fold of the cord.

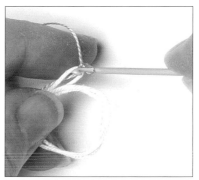

2. Wrap the thread, from back to front, over the hook. Pull the loop through the cord.

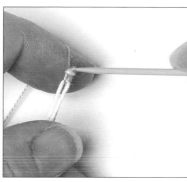

3. Complete a single crochet to anchor the thread to the cord.

4. Loop the cord in a counterclockwise direction to form a circle.

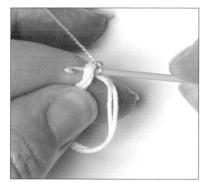

5. Round 1. Take the hook, from front to back, through the circle.

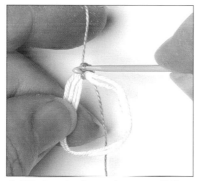

6. Work a single crochet over all four strands of cord.

7. Continue working the required number of single crochet stitches in the same manner (we have worked fifteen more stitches).

8. Pull the end of the cord to close the circle and make it as small as possible.

9. Keeping the cord behind, work a slip stitch into the first single crochet.

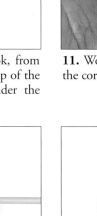

10. Round 2. Take the hook, from front to back, through the top of the next single crochet and under the cord.

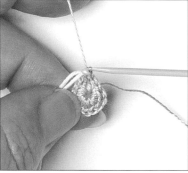

11. Work a single crochet that encases the cord.

12. Repeat steps 10–11 until reaching the end of the round. Keeping the cord behind, work a slip stitch into the first single crochet in the same manner as before.

13. Subsequent rounds. Continue working the required number of rounds in the same manner, adding increases where indicated by your pattern.

HINTS
Irish crochet

The foundation cord should be about twice the thickness of your working thread.

Use the foundation cord to shape your motifs and ensure your stitches lie flat.

When combining lines and circles, flip the line over before slip stitching into the circular motif if you want it to curve in the opposite direction.

More stitches and techniques

Working over a foundation cord: line

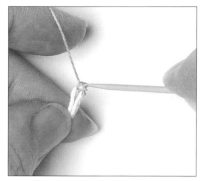

1. Following steps 1–3 on page 95, anchor the thread to the cord.

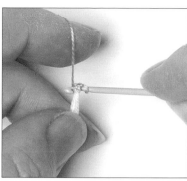

2. Take the hook, from front to back, under the cord. Wrap the thread, from back to front, over the hook.

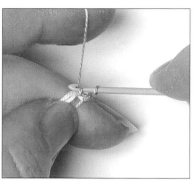

3. Pull the loop to the front of the cord.

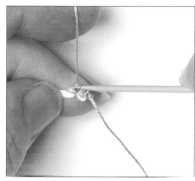

4. Complete a single crochet.

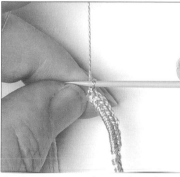

5. Continue working the desired number of single crochet stitches along the cord in the same manner. Make sure the stitches encase cord.

6. Work one chain and turn your work.

7. Work a single crochet into the top of each single crochet of the previous row.

8. Pull the end of the cord to close up the stitches.

9. Shape the line into the desired shape.

Combining circles and lines

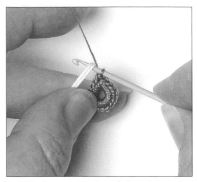

1. Work a circle following the instructions on pages 95–96. Take the hook, from front to back, under the cord only.

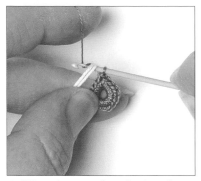

2. Wrap the yarn, from back to front, over the hook.

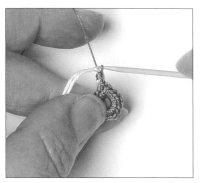

3. Pull the loop to the front of the cord and complete a single crochet.

4. Work a line following steps 5–7 on page 97.

5. Work a slip stitch into the closest stitch of the circle.

6. Pull the end of the cord to close up the stitches and shape the line into the desired shape.

Joining motifs

1. With right sides facing you, arrange the motifs.

2. Making small stitches and using the working thread, stitch the motifs together at the points at which they touch.

3. Weave the ends of cord into the back of their motifs and trim.

Working the background mesh

Note: Instructions for the mesh we have used are given below. However, different mesh patterns can be used. Your pattern will give you instructions.

Mesh pattern

Foundation chain.
Multiple of 25 plus 2.

Row 1. Skip 1 ch, work 1 sc. *Work 2 ch, 1 picot (5 ch, sl st into first ch), 3 ch, 1 picot, 2 ch, skip 7 ch, 1 sc into next ch. Repeat from * to the end of the row.

Row 2. Turn. Work 10 ch, 1 picot, 2 ch, 1 sc in the next 3-ch space between picots of the previous row. *Work 2 ch, 1 picot, 3 ch, 1 picot, 2 ch, 1 sc in the 3-ch space. Repeat from * to the end of the row.

Row 3. Turn. Work 2 ch, 1 picot, 3 ch, 1 picot, 3 ch, 1 picot, 2 ch, 1 sc in 3-ch space. *Work 2 ch, 1 picot, 3 ch, 1 picot, 2 ch, 1 sc in the 3-ch space. Repeat from * to the last sc. Work the last sc into the 10-ch space of the previous row.

Subsequent rows.
Repeat rows 2 and 3.

Last row. Connect the diamonds along the remaining edges with *8 ch, 1 sc in each 3-ch space. Repeat from * to the end.

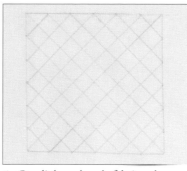

1. On light-colored fabric, draw a diagonal grid the same size as your finished piece. Place the lines the same distance apart as you want the lines of your mesh to be.

3. Work the required number of foundation chains to fit across the base of your grid.

5. With the right side uppermost, position the mesh on the lower edge of the grid. Tack in place along the outside edges. The lines of mesh should align with the grid lines.

2. With right sides facing you, arrange the motifs on the grid. Tack the centers of the motifs to the fabric. Make sure the edges are free.

4. Holding the crochet freely in your hand, work the rows up until just below the lowest motif. Finish with a right-side row.

6. Turn the fabric upside down. Pulling the mesh away from the fabric slightly, crochet toward the motif.

Wide stripes This method helps to prevent large loops of yarn forming on the side of your work.

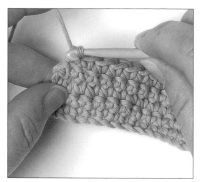

1. Using your first color, work the foundation chain and the desired number of rows up to the last stitch.

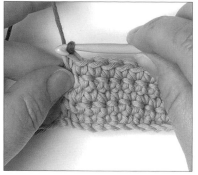

2. Join the new yarn following steps 2–4 on page 101.

3. Work two rows of your second stripe. Take your working yarn, from back to front, under the yarn of the first stripe.

4. Work your turning chain, turn your work, and work two more rows of your second stripe. Take your working yarn, from back to front, under the yarn of the first stripe.

5. Complete the stripe, catching the yarn of the first stripe after every second row.

HINTS

Stripes

If you change color after every row or use an odd number of rows for each stripe, you will need to fasten off the yarn rather than carrying it up the side of your work.

Choose yarns that have similar care requirements and are similar weights.

When fastening off threads, make sure you weave a tail through the crocheted fabric of the same color.

6. To work the next stripe, change yarn color in the same manner as for basic stripes on page 101.

7. Continue working rows in the same manner, carrying the yarns up the side of the work.

More stitches and techniques

Surface Crochet

Surface crochet is most effective when worked on a mesh background. The stitches are worked with the right side of the mesh facing you.

Mesh background

Other stitches besides a mesh can be used as a background, but do not work the stitches too firmly.

1. Work the foundation chain, making sure it is a multiple of two plus six.

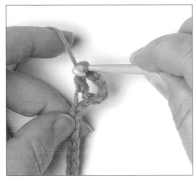

2. Row 1. Skip five chains and work a double crochet into the next chain.

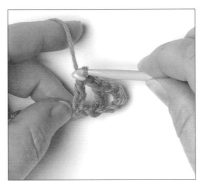

3. Work one chain, skip one chain, and work a double crochet into the next chain.

4. Repeat step 3 to the end of the row.

5. Work four turning chains. Turn your work.

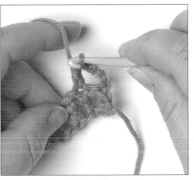

6. Row 2. Skip the first double crochet of the previous row and work a double crochet into the next double crochet.

7. Work one chain, skip one chain in the previous row, and work one double crochet into the next double crochet of the previous row.

8. Repeat step 7 to the end of the row, working the last double crochet into the top of the turning chains (the second chain).

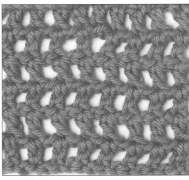

9. Subsequent rows. Repeat steps 5–8 until your fabric is the desired length.

Working vertical lines

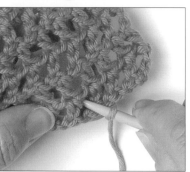 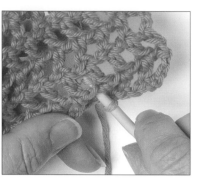 

1. Work a slipknot and place it on the hook. Take the hook, from front to back, through a hole in the mesh near the lower edge. Hold the yarn behind the mesh.

2. Take the yarn, from back to front, over the hook.

3. Pull the loop through both the mesh and the loop on the hook to form a slip stitch.

4. Take the hook, from front to back, through the hole directly above.

5. Repeat steps 2–3 to form a second slip stitch.

6. Continue working stitches in the same manner to the top.

Working horizontal lines

1. Work a slipknot and place it on the hook. Take the hook, from front to back, through a hole in the mesh near the right-hand side. Hold the yarn behind the mesh.

2. Take the yarn, from back to front, over the hook.

3. Pull the loop through both the mesh and the loop on the hook to form a slip stitch.

4. Take the hook, from front to back, through the next hole to the left.

5. Repeat steps 2–3 to form a second slip stitch.

6. Continue working stitches in the same manner to the opposite side.

Working diagonal lines

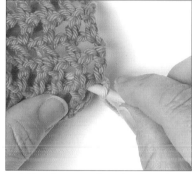

1. Work a slipknot and place it on the hook. Take the hook, from front to back, through a hole in the mesh near the lower right corner. Hold the yarn behind the mesh.

2. Take the yarn, from back to front, over the hook.

3. Pull the loop through both the mesh and the loop on the hook to form a slip stitch.

4. Take the hook, from front to back, through the next hole diagonally above and to the left.

5. Repeat steps 2–3 to form a second slip stitch.

6. Continue working stitches in the same manner to the top.

More stitches and techniques

Tubular Crochet
Tubes are started in the same manner as circular crochet, but each round is worked with exactly the same number of stitches.

Working in rounds

1. Work a slipknot using method 1 on page 12 and place it on the hook. Work a foundation chain of the required number of stitches.

2. Take the hook, from front to back, through the middle of the first chain.

3. Wrap the yarn, from back to front, over the hook.

4. Draw the hook backward to pull the loop through both loops on the hook, forming a slip stitch.

5. Gently pull the dangling tail of yarn to tighten the first stitch.

6. Round 1. Work the required number of turning chains for your stitch (we have worked three chains because our sample uses dc stitch).

7. Work a stitch into each foundation chain until reaching the beginning.

8. Work a slip stitch into the top turning chain to join the round.

9. Subsequent rounds. Working into the top of the stitches of the previous row each time, work all rounds in the same manner as round 1. Fasten off the yarn.

Working in a spiral

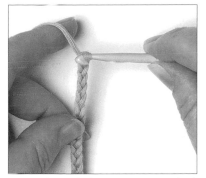

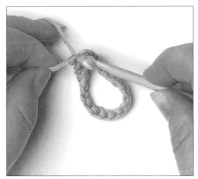

1. Work a slipknot using method 1 on page 12 and place it on the hook. Work a foundation chain of the required number of stitches.

2. Join the foundation chain into a circle following steps 2–4 on page 106.

3. Gently pull the dangling tail of yarn to tighten the first stitch.

4. Work a single crochet into the first foundation chain.

5. Continue working a single crochet into each foundation chain until reaching the beginning.

6. Work a single crochet into the first single crochet you worked.

7. Place a stitch marker into the single crochet just worked.

8. Continue working a single crochet into the top of each single crochet until reaching the stitch with the marker.

9. Remove the marker and work a single crochet into the stitch.

10. Replace the marker into the stitch just worked.

11. Repeat steps 8–10 until the tube is the desired length.

12. Remove the marker. Work a slip stitch into the marked stitch and fasten off the yarn following the instructions on page 24.

Afghan Crochet

Also known as Tunisian crochet, tricot crochet, and shepherd's knitting, this interesting technique is really a cross between knitting and crochet. It is worked with a tool that has the tip of a crochet hook and the shaft and end of a knitting needle. Unlike other forms of crochet, you do not reverse the work after each row so you always have the right side facing you.

Basic stitch

It takes two rows of stitching—one picking-up row and one fastening-off row—to form one row of stitches.

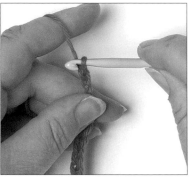

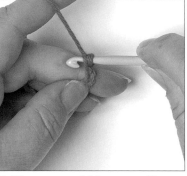

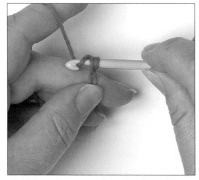

1. Using a hook one size smaller than the one you will use for the piece, work a foundation chain of the required number of stitches plus one.

2. First row: picking up. Change hook. Take the hook through the top loop of the second chain.

3. Wrap the yarn, from back to front, over the hook.

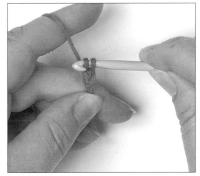

4. Draw the hook backward to pull a loop of yarn through the chain.

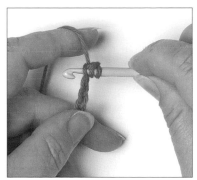

5. Leave the new loop on the hook and take the hook through the top loop of the next chain.

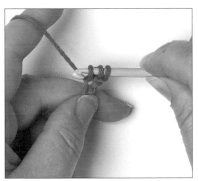

6. Repeat steps 3–4 to form a second loop.

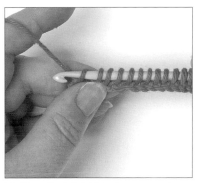

7. Continue picking up a loop through each chain stitch in the same manner to the end of the foundation chain.

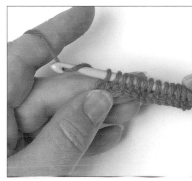

8. First row: fastening off. Wrap the yarn, from back to front, over the hook.

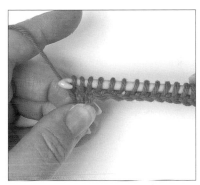

9. Draw the hook backward to pull the new wrap through the first loop on the hook.

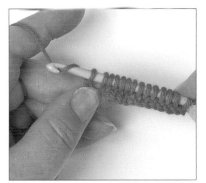

10. Again, wrap the yarn, from back to front, over the hook.

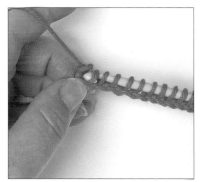

11. Draw the hook backward to pull the new wrap through the first two loops on the hook.

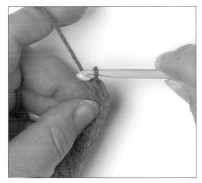

12. Repeat until only one loop remains on the hook.

More stitches and techniques

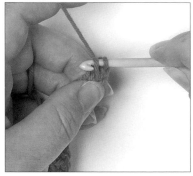

13. Second row: picking up. Take the hook, from right to left, behind the second vertical bar of the previous row.

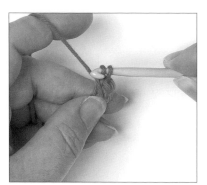

14. Wrap the yarn, from back to front, over the hook. Draw the hook backward to pull the wrap behind the vertical bar. There are two loops on the hook.

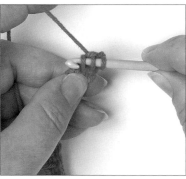

15. Take the hook, from right to left, behind the next vertical bar of the previous row.

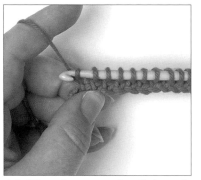

16. Wrap the yarn and pull through as before. Continue in the same manner to the end of the row.

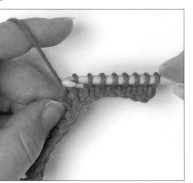

17. Second row: fastening off. Work in exactly the same manner as the first fastening-off row.

18. Subsequent rows. Repeat steps 13–17 until the work is the required length. Fasten off following the instructions on page 24.

HINTS

Afghan crochet

Afghan crochet makes a very firm, thick fabric. Unlike other types of crochet and knitting, it can be cut without it unraveling.

Make sure your hook is long enough to hold all the stitches required to cover the width of your piece.

Pull the yarn firmly when working the first pick-up stitch of each row. This helps to maintain neat edges.

Work single crochet across your last row of afghan crochet to neaten and strengthen the top edge.

Take care when blocking as the fabric has a tendency to pull on the bias.

Afghan crochet has a tendency to curl unless you add a border.

More stitches and techniques

Afghan stockinette stitch

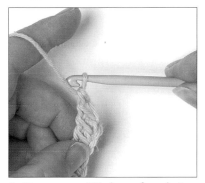

1. Base row. Work a foundation chain of the required number of stitches plus one and then work the first row as for the first row of basic stitch on pages 108–109.

2. Second row: picking up. Work a single chain. Take the hook, from front to back, through the middle of the loop of the second stitch.

3. Wrap the yarn, from back to front, over the hook.

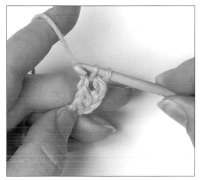

4. Draw the hook backward to pull the wrap through and form a loop on the hook.

5. Take the hook, from front to back, through the middle of the loop of the next stitch.

6. Complete the stitch following steps 3–4.

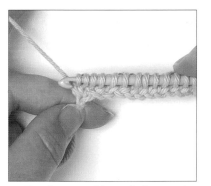

7. Continue working stitches to the end of the row in the same manner.

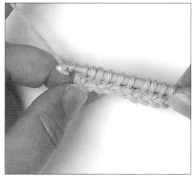

8. Second row: fastening off. Wrap the yarn, from back to front, over the hook.

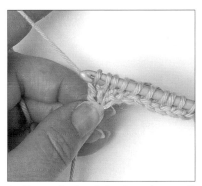

9. Draw the hook backward to pull the new wrap through the first loop on the hook.

10. Again, wrap the yarn, from back to front, over the hook.

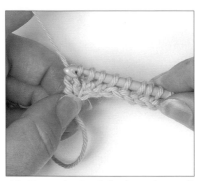

11. Draw the hook backward to pull the new wrap through the first two loops on the hook.

12. Repeat steps 10–11 until only one loop remains on the hook.

13. Subsequent rows. Repeat steps 2–12 until the work is the required length. Fasten off following the instructions on page 24.

Afghan purl stitch

This stitch is similar in appearance to knitting's garter stitch.

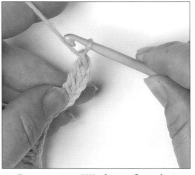

1. Base row. Work a foundation chain of the required number of stitches plus one and then work the first row as for the first row of basic stitch on pages 108–109.

2. Second row: picking up. Work a single chain. With the yarn at the front, take the hook, from right to left, behind the second vertical bar of the previous row.

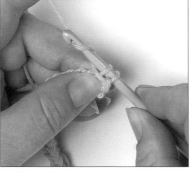

3. Wrap the yarn around the hook in a clockwise direction.

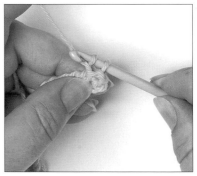

4. Draw the hook backward to pull the wrap through and form a loop on the hook.

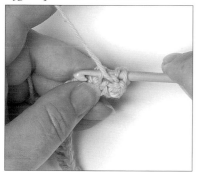

5. Again, with the yarn at the front, take the hook, from right to left, behind the next vertical bar of the previous row.

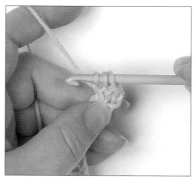

6. Complete the stitch following steps 3–4.

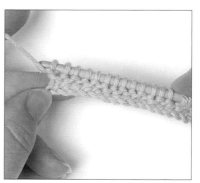

7. Continue working stitches to the end of the row in the same manner.

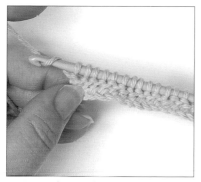

8. Second row: fastening off. Wrap the yarn, from back to front, over the hook

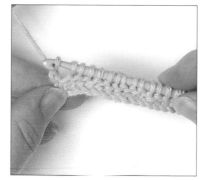

9. Draw the hook backward to pull the new wrap through the first loop on the hook.

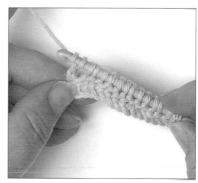

10. Again, wrap the yarn, from back to front, over the hook.

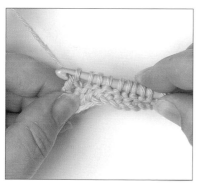

11. Draw the hook backward to pull the new wrap through the first two loops on the hook.

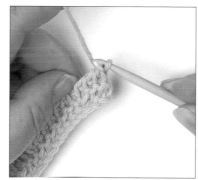

12. Repeat steps 10–11 until only one loop remains on the hook.

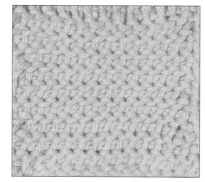

13. Subsequent rows. Repeat steps 2–12 until the work is the required length. Fasten off following the instructions on page 24.

More stitches and techniques

Afghan crossed stitch

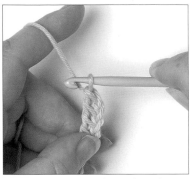

1. Base row. Work a foundation chain of an odd number of stitches and then work the first row as for the first row of basic stitch on pages 108–109.

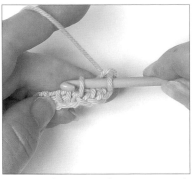

2. Second row: picking up. Work a single chain. Take the hook, from right to left, behind the third vertical bar of the previous row.

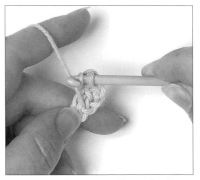

3. Wrap the yarn, from back to front, over the hook. Draw the hook backward to pull the wrap through and form a loop on the hook.

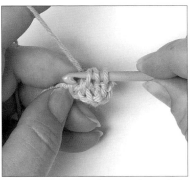

4. Take the hook, from right to left, behind the second vertical bar of the previous row.

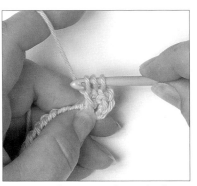

5. Wrap the yarn, from back to front, over the hook. Draw the hook backward to pull the wrap through and form a loop on the hook.

6. Skip one vertical bar and take the hook, from right to left, behind the next vertical bar of the previous row.

7. Wrap the yarn and form a loop on the hook as before.

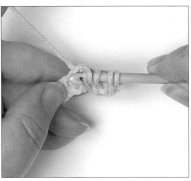

8. Take the hook, from right to left, behind the skipped vertical bar of the previous row.

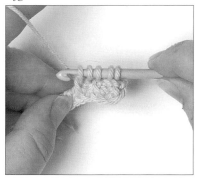

9. Wrap the yarn and form a loop on the hook as before.

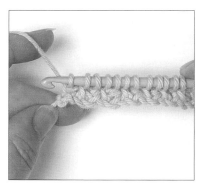

10. Repeating steps 6–9, continue working stitches to the end of the row.

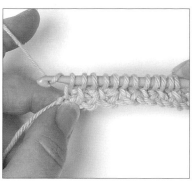

11. Second row: fastening off. Wrap the yarn, from back to front, over the hook.

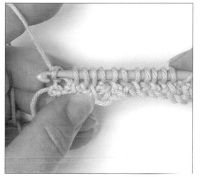

12. Draw the hook backward to pull the new wrap through the first loop on the hook.

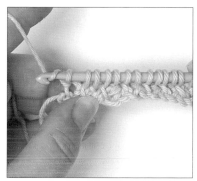

13. Again, wrap the yarn, from back to front, over the hook.

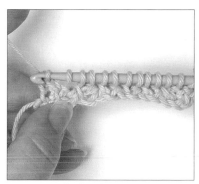

14. Draw the hook backward to pull the new wrap through the first two loops on the hook.

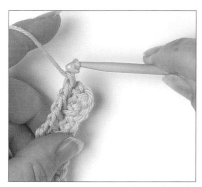

15. Repeat steps 13–14 until only one loop remains on the hook.

16. Subsequent rows. Repeat steps 2–15 until the work is the required length. Fasten off following the instructions on page 24.

Afghan lace stitch

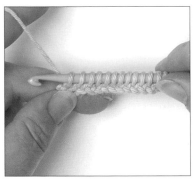

1. Base row. Work a foundation chain, making sure the number of stitches is a multiple of four plus one. Work the first row as for the first picking up row of basic stitch on pages 108–109.

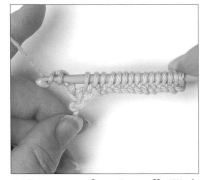

2. Base row: fastening off. Work three chains. Wrap the yarn, from back to front, over the hook.

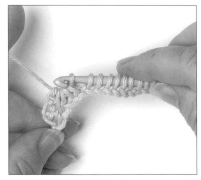

3. Draw the hook backward to pull the wrap through the first five loops on the hook.

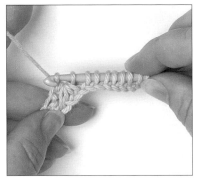

4. Wrap the yarn, from back to front, over the hook.

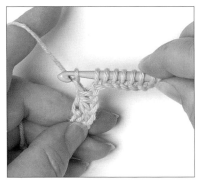

5. Draw the hook backward to pull the wrap through the next loop on the hook.

6. Repeat steps 2–5 to form a second cluster. Continue to the end of the row in the same manner.

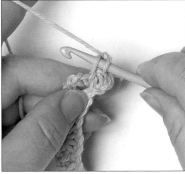

7. Second row: picking up. Work one chain. Take the hook, from front to back, through the loop at the top of the first cluster.

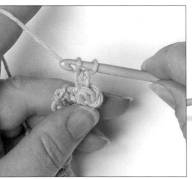

8. Wrap the yarn, from back to front, over the hook. Draw the hook backward to pull the new wrap through the first loop on the hook.

More stitches and techniques

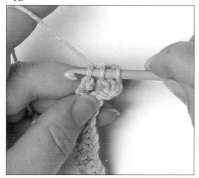

9. Take the hook through the top loop of the first chain.

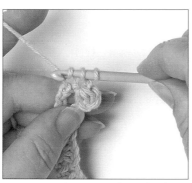

10. Wrap the yarn, from back to front, over the hook. Draw the hook backward to pull the new wrap through the chain.

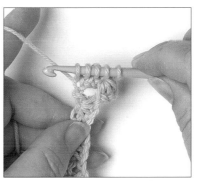

11. Repeat steps 9–10 in the next two chain stitches.

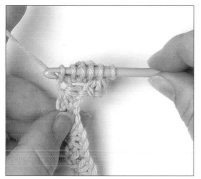

12. Take the hook, from front to back, through the loop at the top of the next cluster. Wrap the yarn and pull the new wrap through as before.

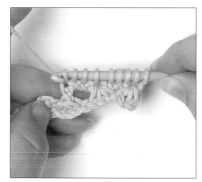

13. Work a stitch into each of the next three chain stitches as before.

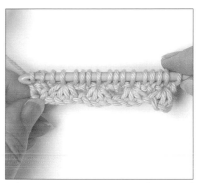

14. Repeat steps 12–13 to the end of the row.

15. Second row: fastening off. Fasten off in the same manner as the base row.

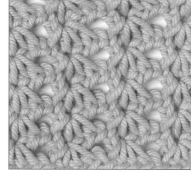

16. Subsequent rows. Repeat steps 7–15 until the work is the required length. Fasten off following the instructions on page 24.

More stitches and techniques

117

Buttons, Buttonholes, and Button Loops

Ring button

These buttons are worked around a plastic ring. Choose a ring that is approximately ⅛" (3 mm) smaller than the desired button size.

1. Make a slipknot and place on hook. With hook in your right hand, wrap the yarn around your left hand (see page 10), then hold the ring between your thumb and middle finger.

2. Take the hook from front to back through the ring.

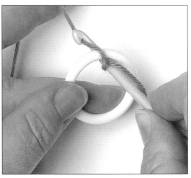

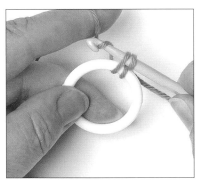

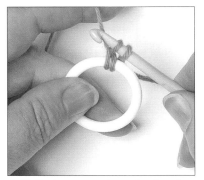

3. Pick up the yarn with the barb of the hook.

4. Pull the yarn through the ring to the front. With the hook along the top of the ring, wrap the yarn, from back to front, over the hook.

5. Pull the yarn through the first loop on the hook. Two loops remain on the hook and there are two loops around the ring.

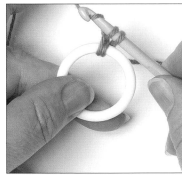

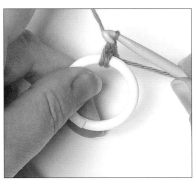

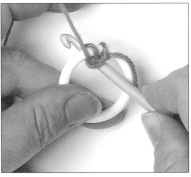

6. Wrap the yarn, from back to front, over the hook.

7. Pull the loop through both loops on the hook to complete a single crochet stitch.

8. Again, take the hook, from front to back, through the ring.

9. Catch the yarn with the barb of the hook and pull it through the ring.

10. Complete the single crochet stitch.

11. Repeat steps 8–10 until the ring is completely covered.

12. Take the hook, from front to back, through the first stitch. Wrap the yarn, from back to front, over the hook.

13. Pull the loop through both the stitch and the loop on the hook to complete a slip stitch.

14. Leaving a tail of yarn approximately 16" (40 cm) long, fasten off the yarn.

15. Thread the tail into a tapestry needle. Take the needle, from back to front, through the outer loop of the next single crochet.

16. Pull the yarn through. Continue working a stitch through the edge of each single crochet stitch in the same manner.

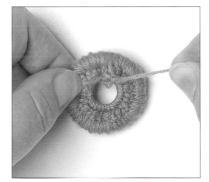

17. Pull the thread firmly and pull the stitches into the middle of the ring.

Added touches

Ring button / continued

18. Tie the two tails of thread together. Cut off the unthreaded tail. Take the needle behind several stitches on one side of the ring.

19. Pull the thread through and take the needle behind several stitches on the opposite side.

20. Work several more stitches that go from side to side and form a star shape on the back of the button.

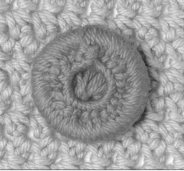

21. Take the needle behind the center of the star.

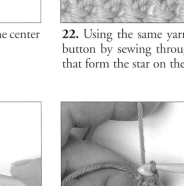

22. Using the same yarn, attach the button by sewing through the yarns that form the star on the back.

HINTS Buttons

Use a smaller hook than what you would normally use with the yarn you are working with.

If you wish, you can insert a small wad of the same yarn the button is made from inside the ball button before closing the back.

Ball button

1. Make a slipknot and place it on the hook. Work three chains.

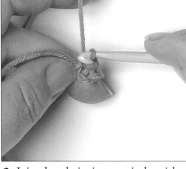

2. Join the chain into a circle with a slip stitch.

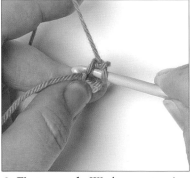

3. First round. Work one turning chain. Take the hook, from front to back, through the ring.

4. Wrap the yarn over the hook and work a single crochet.

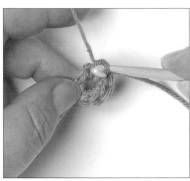

5. Work seven more single crochet stitches in the same manner. Make sure you take the hook through the ring before working each stitch.

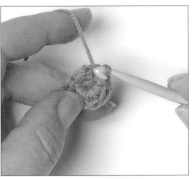

6. Work a slip stitch into the turning chain at the beginning of the round.

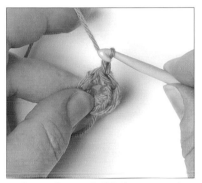

7. Second round. Work one turning chain.

8. Work one single crochet into the next stitch.

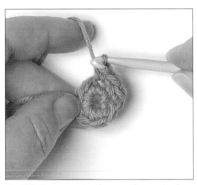

9. Work two single crochet stitches into the next stitch.

10. Repeat steps 8–9 three more times.

11. Work a slip stitch into the turning chain at the beginning of the round.

12. Pull the beginning tail of yarn through the center hole.

Added touches

13. Third round. Work one turning chain.

14. Take the hook, from front to back, through the center hole.

15. Catch the yarn with the barb of the hook and pull through a long loop.

16. Take the yarn, from back to front, over the hook. Pull the yarn through both loops on the hook.

17. Repeat steps 14–16 fifteen times.

18. Work a slip stitch into the turning chain at the beginning of the round.

19. Fourth round. Work one turning chain.

20. Skip one stitch and work a single crochet into the next stitch.

21. Continue in this manner, working a single crochet into every second stitch.

22. Work a slip stitch into the turning chain at the beginning of the round.

23. Leaving a tail of yarn approx-imately 16" (40 cm) long, fasten off the yarn.

24. Complete the button following steps 15–17 on page 119. Tuck the unthreaded tail of yarn inside the button.

25. Secure the yarn with two small backstitches.

26. Attach the button using the same tail of yarn.

Horizontal buttonhole with single crochet

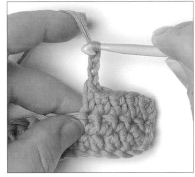

1. On a right-side row, work single crochet to the beginning of the buttonhole.

2. Work enough chain stitches to almost cover the diameter of the button.

3. Skip the same number of single crochet stitches in the previous row (that is, if you worked three chains, skip three stitches) and work a single crochet into the next stitch.

Added touches

4. Continue in single crochet to the end of the row or to the position for the next buttonhole.

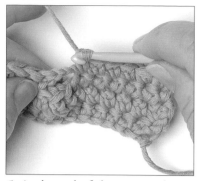

5. At the end of the row, work one turning chain. Turn your work and stitch to the beginning of the buttonhole with single crochet.

6. Take the hook, from front to back, through the buttonhole.

7. Take the yarn, from back to front, over the hook and pull the loop through.

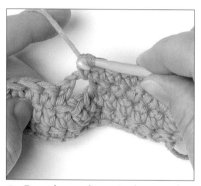

8. Complete the single crochet stitch.

9. Repeat steps 6–8 until you have worked the same number of single crochet stitches as there were chain stitches in the previous row.

10. Continue in single crochet to the end of the row or to the position for the next buttonhole.

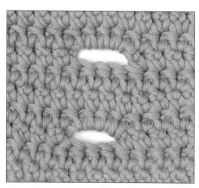

11. Continue working the required number of rows beyond the buttonhole row.

HINTS
Buttonholes

Buttonholes worked with single crochet are generally stronger and neater than those worked with longer stitches.

Horizontal buttonhole with double crochet

1. On a right-side row, work double crochet to the beginning of the buttonhole.

2. Take the hook, from top to bottom, behind the diagonal strand of yarn halfway down the last worked stitch.

3. Take the yarn, from back to front, over the hook.

4. Draw the hook backward to pull the loop through.

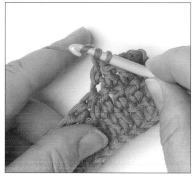

5. Again, take the yarn, from back to front, over the hook.

6. Pull the yarn through both loops on the hook.

7. Take the hook behind the left strand of yarn at the front of the stitch you just worked.

8. Repeat steps 3–6 to work a second stitch.

9. Continue working stitches in the same manner as the previous stitch until the buttonhole is the desired width.

Horizontal buttonhole with double crochet / continued

10. Take the hook behind the left strand of yarn at the front of the stitch you just worked. Wrap the yarn and pull the loop through.

11. Skip the same number of stitches as you worked for the buttonhole (that is, if you worked three stitches, skip three stitches) and take the hook through the next stitch.

12. Take the yarn, from back to front, over the hook. Draw the loop through.

 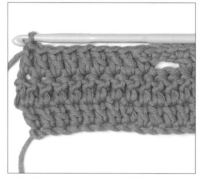 

13. Complete the double crochet stitch.

14. Continue in double crochet stitch to the end of the row or to the position for the next buttonhole.

15. Continue working the required number of rows beyond the buttonhole row.

Vertical buttonhole
This method will work with any stitch. Here we have used single crochet.

1. On a right-side row, work to the position for the buttonhole.

2. Work the turning chain and turn your work. We have worked one turning chain.

3. Continue working rows on this side until it is the same height as the buttonhole you wish to make.

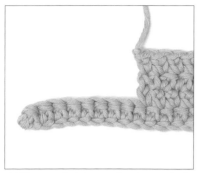

4. If you finish at the buttonhole edge, fasten off the yarn. If you finish at the fabric edge, leave the yarn dangling.

5. Join a new yarn at the base of the buttonhole.

6. Work one turning chain. Continue on this side until it matches the first side. If you finish at the buttonhole, fasten off the yarn. If you finish at the fabric edge, leave the yarn dangling.

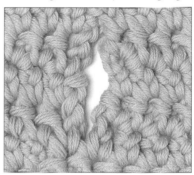

7. Pick up the yarn at the edge of the fabric and work across the row to the buttonhole.

8. Continue stitching across the next section.

9. Continue working the required number of rows beyond the buttonhole row. Fasten off the tails of yarn following the instructions on page 24.

Button loop

1. On a right-side row, work to the end of the position for the button loop.

2. Work enough chain stitches to almost cover the diameter of the button.

3. Remove the hook from the loop. Take the hook, from front to back, through the top of the stitch at the beginning of the button loop.

4. Replace the loop of the last chain on the hook.

5. Pull the loop through the top of the stitch.

6. Take the hook, from front to back, through the top of the next stitch to the right. Take the yarn, from back to front, over the hook.

7. Pull the loop through both the stitch and the loop on the hook.

8. Take the hook, from front to back, through the button loop.

9. Wrap the yarn over the hook and work a single crochet.

10. Repeat steps 8–9 until you have worked the same number of single crochet stitches as you had chains.

11. Work a slip stitch into the stitch where you first started the chain.

12. Continue stitching to the end of the row or to the position for the next button loop.

Cords
Single crochet cord

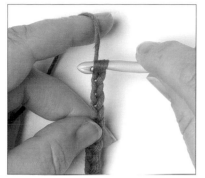

1. Work a foundation chain the length of the cord you wish to make.

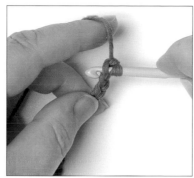

2. Change to a smaller hook. Take the hook, from front to back, through the top of the second chain from the hook. (The hook goes under one strand of yarn.)

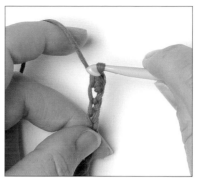

3. Work a single crochet.

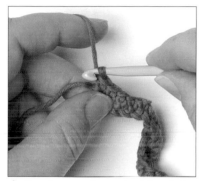

4. Continue to the end of the chain, working a single crochet into each one.

5. Work one turning chain. Turn the cord so the foundation chain is at the top.

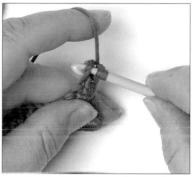

6. Take the hook, from front to back, through the first foundation chain. (The hook goes under two strands of yarn.)

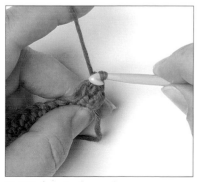

7. Work a single crochet.

8. Work stitches in the same manner to the end of the chain.

9. Fasten off the yarn following the instructions on page 24.

Single slip-stitch cord

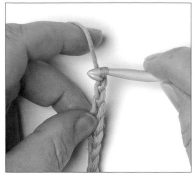

1. Work a foundation chain the length of the cord you wish to make.

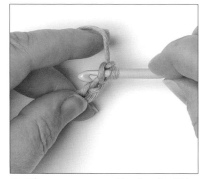

2. Change to a smaller hook. Take the hook, from front to back, through the top of the second chain from the hook. (The hook goes under one strand of yarn.)

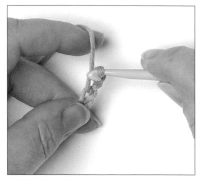

3. Work a slip stitch.

4. Continue to the end of the chain, working a slip stitch into each one.

5. Fasten off the yarn following the instructions on page 24.

HINTS
Cords

Work cords with a firm tension. Using a smaller hook can help you achieve this. If cords are worked too loosely, they will easily pull out of shape.

Double slip-stitch cord

1. Work a foundation chain the length of the cord you wish to make.

2. Change to a smaller hook. Work slip stitch along the top of the chain in the same manner as for the single slip-stitch cord above.

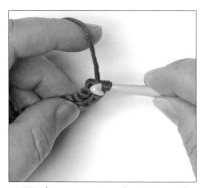

3. Work one turning chain. Turn the cord so the foundation chain is at the top.

Double slip-stitch cord / continued

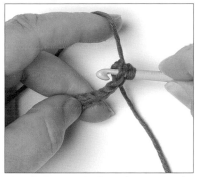

4. Take the hook, from front to back, through the first foundation chain. (The hook goes under two strands of yarn.)

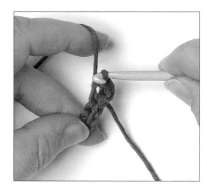

5. Work a slip stitch.

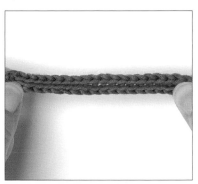

6. Work slip stitches in the same manner to the end of the chain. Fasten off the yarn following the instructions on page 24.

Edgings

Edgings usually have one straight edge and one shaped edge.

Edging 1

Foundation: Work a foundation chain to the desired length, making sure it is a multiple of 14 plus 5 ch.

Row 1: Turn your work. Skip first ch and then work 1 sc into each ch. Work 3 turning chains.

Row 2: Turn your work. Work 1 dc into each of next 3 sc. *Work 3 ch, skip 3 sc, work 1 dc into each of the next 4 sc. Repeat from *, ending with 3 ch and 4 dc. Work 4 turning chains.

Row 3: Turn your work. Work 4 dc into the 3-ch space. *Work 4 ch, 4 dc into next space. Repeat from *, ending with 3 ch, 1 dc into the last dc of the previous row.

Row 4: Turn your work. Work 1 sc, 3 ch, 1 sc into first space. *Work 3 ch, then into next space work 1 tr, 4 ch, 1 sc into fourth ch (forming a picot), 1 tr, 1 picot, 1 dtr, 1 picot, 1 dtr, 1 picot, 1 tr, 1 picot, 1 tr, 1 picot, 3 ch, into next space work 1 sc, 3 ch, 1 sc. Repeat from * to end of row.

Double Triple Crochet Stitch (dtr)

1. *Yarn over three times.*
2. *Yarn over and draw up a loop.*
3. *(Yarn over and pull through two loops) four times.*

Edging 2

Foundation: Work a foundation chain to the desired length, making sure it is a multiple of 7 plus 1 ch.

Row 1: Turn your work. Skip the first ch and then work 1 sc into each ch. Work 5 turning chains.

Row 2: Turn your work. *Work 2 dtr into the first sc, leaving the last stitch of each dtr on the hook. *Skip 5 sc, work 2 dtr into next sc leaving 5 stitches on hook, draw hook through all 5 stitches at the same time, work 5 ch, 1 sl st into the same place as last 2 dtr, 5 ch, 2 dtr into the same place, leaving 3 stitches on hook. Repeat from * ending with skip 5 sc, work 3 dtr into next stitch, leaving 6 stitches on hook, draw hook through all 6 stitches at the same time. Work 5 turning chains.

Row 3: Turn your work. Into the stitch of the cluster, work 2 dtr together. *Work 5 ch, 1 sl st into first ch (forming a picot), 4 more picots, 3 dtr into the same place, leaving 4 stitches on hook. Into the next cluster, work 3 dtr, leaving 7 stitches on hook, draw hook through all 7 stitches at the same time. Repeat from *, ending with 5 picots, 3 dtr together.

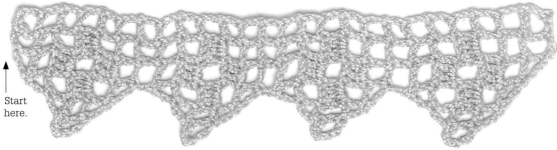

Start here.

Edging 3 (worked sideways)

Foundation: Work a foundation chain of 14 ch.

Row 1: Work 1 dc into the eighth ch from the hook, 2 ch, skip 2 ch, 1 dc, 2 ch, skip 2 ch, 1 dc. Work 5 turning chains. *Note: 2 ch, skip 2 ch, 1 dc makes one space.*

Row 2: Turn your work. Work 1 dc into next dc, 2 spaces, 2 ch, 1 tr into the base of the last dc. Work 6 turning chains.

Row 3: Turn your work. Work 1 dc into tr, 1 space, 2 dc into space, 1 dc, 2 spaces. Work 5 turning chains.

Row 4: Turn your work. Work 1 dc into next dc, 2 dc into space, 1 dc, 1 space, 2 dc into space, 1 dc, 1 space, 2 ch, 1 tr into the base of the last dc.

Row 5: Turn your work. Work sl st to the first dc, 3 ch, 1 dc into next dc, 1 space, 2 dc into space, 1 dc, 2 spaces. Work 5 turning chains.

Row 6: Turn your work. Work 1 dc into next dc, 2 spaces, 1 tr into next dc. Work 5 turning chains.

Row 7: Turn your work. Work 1 dc into next dc, 2 spaces.

Subsequent rows: Turn your work. Repeat rows 2–7 until the edging is the desired length.

Added touches

Edging 4

Foundation: Work a foundation chain to the desired length, making sure it is a multiple of 8 plus 5 ch.

Row 1: Skip 3 ch and then work 1 dc into each ch. Work 4 turning chains.

Row 2: Turn your work. *Skip 1 dc, 1 dc into next, 1 ch. Repeat from * to the end of the row.

Row 3: Turn your work. Into the first space, work 1 sc, 1 ch, 1 sc. *Work 5 ch, skip 1 space, into the next space work 3 tr, leaving the last stitch of each on hook, draw hook through all 4 stitches at the same time, work 5 ch, 1 sl st into top of tr (forming a picot), 5 ch, skip 1 space, work 1 sc, 3 ch, 1 sc into next space. Repeat from * to end of row.

Fringes
Single-knot fringe

1. Wrap the yarn around a piece of card the same height as the desired length of the fringe plus ⅜" (1 cm). Cut through the strands at one end.

2. Place several strands together (your pattern will often specify how many) and fold them in half.

3. Using a large hook, take it, from front to back, through the edge of your crocheted fabric.

4. Hook the fold of the strands with the barb of the hook.

5. Pull the strands partway through the fabric. A loop will form.

6. Catch the ends of the strands with the hook and pull them through the loop.

7. Pull on the ends of the strands to tighten the loop near the fabric edge.

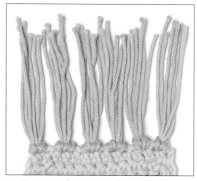

8. Repeat the procedure along the edge of the fabric at the desired intervals.

9. Trim the ends of the strands so they are even.

Double-knot fringe

1. Wrap the yarn around a piece of card the same height as the desired length of the fringe plus approximately 1⅛" (3 cm). Cut through the strands at one end.

2. Following steps 2–8 on page 134, work a single-knot fringe along the edge of the crocheted fabric.

3. Pick up half of the strands from the first piece of fringing and half from the second piece.

4. Loosely wrap the strands around your left index finger.

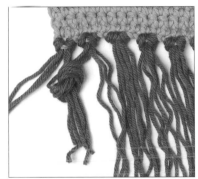

5. Take the ends through the loop.

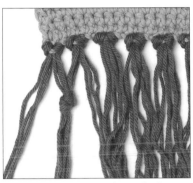

6. Pull the ends to tighten the loop.

7. Repeat the procedure along the edge of the fabric, picking up the remaining strands from one piece of fringing and half the strands of the adjacent piece each time.

8. Trim the ends of the strands so they are even.

Chain fringe

Chain fringe This fringe can be worked along the edge of your crocheted fabric, or it can be worked as a detached fringe that can be joined on later.

1. With the right side facing you, work a row of single crochet. Make sure the number of stitches is a multiple of three plus one.

2. Work one turning chain and turn your work. Work a single crochet into the first stitch of the previous row.

3. Work seven chains.

4. Skip two stitches and then work a single crochet.

5. Repeat steps 3–4 to the end of the row.

6. Work one turning chain and turn your work. Work a single crochet into the first stitch of the previous row.

7. Work eleven chains.

8. Work a single crochet into the next single crochet of the previous row.

9. Repeat steps 7–8 to the end of the row.

10. Work one turning chain and turn your work. Work a single crochet into the first stitch of the previous row.

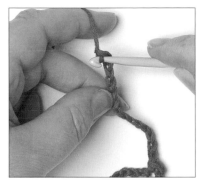

11. Work fifteen chains.

12. Work a single crochet into the next single crochet of the previous row.

13. Repeat steps 11–12 to the end of the row.

14. Work one turning chain and turn your work. Work a single crochet into the first stitch of the previous row.

15. Work nineteen chains.

16. Work a single crochet into the next single crochet of the previous row.

17. Repeat steps 15–16 to the end of the row.

18. Fasten off the yarn following the instructions on page 24.

Added touches

137

Corkscrew fringe

1. With the right side facing you, work a row of single crochet. Turn your work.

2. Work seventeen chains.

3. Work a single crochet into the second chain from the hook.

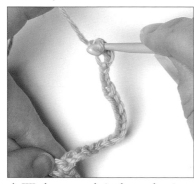

4. Work a second single crochet into the same chain.

5. Continue working two single crochet stitches into each chain until reaching the end of the chains.

6. Work a slip stitch into the next single crochet of the previous row.

7. Repeat steps 2–6 to the end of the row.

8. Fasten off the yarn following the instructions on page 24.

instructions on page 24.

HINTS
Fringes

For a different look, vary the lengths of your corkscrews in a corkscrew fringe by varying the number of chains you use for each one.

Use fine yarn or thread for a chain fringe to create a delicate and lacy look.

Added touches

Spirals Basic spiral

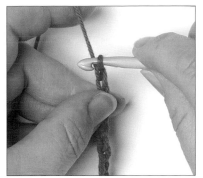

1. Work a foundation chain the length of the spiral you want to make plus three turning chains.

2. Change to a smaller hook. Work a double crochet into the fourth chain from the hook.

3. Work two more double crochet stitches into the same chain.

4. Work four double crochet stitches into the next chain.

5. Continue working four double crochet stitches into each chain to the end of the foundation chain.

6. Fasten off the yarn following the instructions on page 24, but leave a tail long enough to attach the spiral to your chosen project.

Multicolored spiral

1. Work a basic spiral following the instructions above.

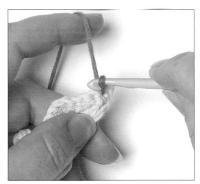

2. Join a new yarn to the end of the spiral at the outer edge.

3. Work single crochet along the outer edge. Fasten off the yarn following the instructions on page 24.

Work the foundation chain with a fairly loose tension.

Spirals can also be made with other stitches from the double crochet family. Remember to adjust the number of turning chains to suit your selected stitch.

Added touches

Three-Dimensional Flowers: Star flower

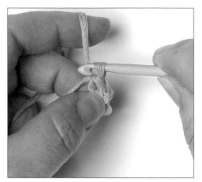

1. Begin with a slipknot and work three chains. Join the chains into a circle by working a slip stitch through the first chain.

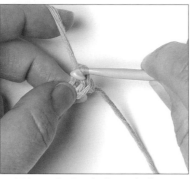

2. Taking the hook through the ring, work a single crochet.

3. Work ten chains.

4. Work a single crochet into the third chain from the hook.

5. Work a hdc into the next chain, a dc into the next chain, a triple crochet into each of the next two chains, a dc into the next chain, a hdc into the next chain and a single crochet into the last chain.

6. Repeat steps 2–5 four more times. You will have five petals.

7. Work a slip stitch into the very first single crochet that you worked.

8. Fasten off the yarn but do not trim the tails (these can be used to attach the flower).

Bell flower

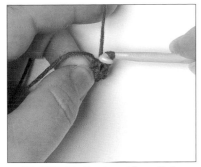

1. FLOWER. Begin with a slipknot and work three chains. Join the chains into a circle by working a slip stitch through the first chain.

2. Round 1. Work four chains. Work eleven tr stitches, taking the hook through the circle each time. Work a slip stitch into the fourth chain at the beginning of the rnd.

3. Round 2. Work four chains, then work a triple crochet into the same place as the slip stitch.

4. Work a triple crochet into each of the next two triple crochet stitches of the previous round. Work two triple crochet stitches into the next triple crochet of the previous round.

5. Repeat step 4, finishing with a triple crochet into each of the last two stitches. Work a slip stitch into the fourth chain at the beginning of the round.

6. Round 3. Work a single crochet into the same place as the last slip stitch and then one single crochet into each triple crochet of the previous round. Work a slip stitch into the first single crochet of the round.

7. Round 4. Work a single crochet into each single crochet of the previous round. Work a slip stitch into the first single crochet of the round.

8. Round 5. Work a single crochet into the first single crochet of the previous round. Work three chains, then a single crochet into the second single crochet of the previous round.

9. Work three chains. Continue working a single crochet into each single crochet of the previous round with three chains in between.

10. Finish with a slip stitch into the first single crochet of the round. Fasten off the yarn.

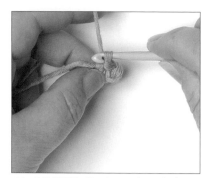

11. LEAVES. Begin with a slipknot and work three chains. Join the chains into a circle by working a slip stitch through the first chain.

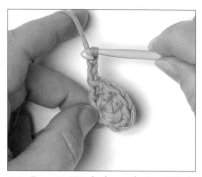

12. Row 1. Work three chains. Work four double crochet stitches, taking the hook through the circle each time. Work three turning chains.

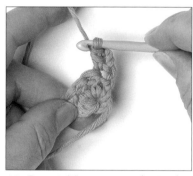

13. Row 2. Turn your work. Work a double crochet into the first double crochet of the previous row.

14. Work a double crochet into each double crochet of the previous row and then two double crochet stitches into the top of the turning chain. Work three turning chains.

15. Row 3. Turn your work. Work a dc into every dc of the previous row, including the first one. Work two dc into the top of the turning chain. Work three turning chains.

16. Row 4. Turn your work. Skip the first dc of the previous row and work a dc into all remaining dc. Work one dc into the top of the turning chain of the previous row. Work three turning chains.

17. Row 5. Turn your work. Double crochet two together (see page 32), work three double crochet stitches, double crochet two together. Work three turning chains.

Bell flower / continued

18. Row 6. Turn your work. Double crochet two together, work one double crochet, double crochet two together. Work three turning chains.

19. Row 7. Turn your work. Double crochet three together (see page 33), work one double crochet. Work one chain.

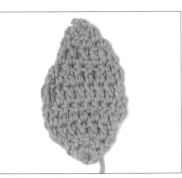

20. Fasten off the yarn.

21. Work a second leaf in the same manner as the first leaf.

22. ASSEMBLING THE FLOWER. Aligning circles, place the two leaves together so they slightly overlap.

23. Flatten the base of the flower and position it over the circles of the leaves. Using the tail of yarn at the base of the flower, stitch the base of the flower and the ends of the leaves together.

24. Shape the flower with the tips of your fingers.

Added touches

143

Edge Finishes
Edge finishes are worked from the crocheted fabric outward.

Crab stitch
Crab stitch is also known as reverse single crochet and it is worked in the opposite direction to single crochet.

1. With the right side facing you, work a row of single crochet along the edge of the crocheted fabric. Make sure the stitches are evenly spaced.

2. Change to a smaller hook. Twist the hook so the barb end is pointing downward.

3. Take the hook, from front to back, through the next stitch to the right.

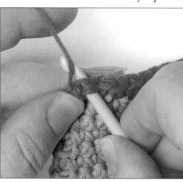

4. Catch the yarn in the barb of the hook.

5. Pull the yarn through the stitch, again twisting the hook so the barb end is pointing downward.

6. Return the hook to its normal position. There are two loops on the hook.

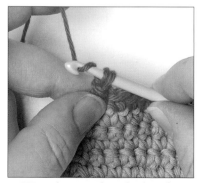

7. Wrap the yarn, from back to front, over the hook.

8. Pull the loop through both loops on the hook. One loop remains.

9. Again, twist the hook so the barb points downward.

Crab stitch / continued

10. Work a second stitch following steps 3–8.

11. Continue working stitches to the end of the row in the same manner.

HINTS
Edge finishes

A row of single crochet is an excellent base for virtually any edge finish.

When working crab stitch in the round, there is no need to work an extra chain at any corners, because the stitch is very flexible.

You can vary the size and spacing of your shells in a shell edge. Work out how many stitches in your pattern repeat. Make sure the number of single crochet in your base row is a multiple of this number plus one.

Shell edge

1. With the wrong side of the fabric facing you, work a row of single crochet along the edge of the crocheted fabric. Make sure the number of single crochet stitches is a multiple of four plus one.

2. Work one turning chain and turn your work.

3. Work a single crochet into the first single crochet of the previous row.

4. Skip one stitch and then work five double crochet stitches into the next stitch.

5. Skip one stitch and then work a single crochet into the next stitch.

6. Repeat steps 4–5 to the end of the row.

Dainty picot edge

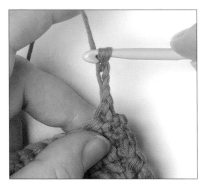

1. With the wrong side facing you, work a row of single crochet along the edge of the crocheted fabric. Make sure you have an even number of stitches.

2. Turn your work and work three chains.

3. Take the hook through the back of the third chain from the hook.

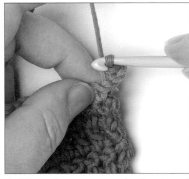

4. Wrap the yarn over the hook and pull through both loops on the hook to form a slip stitch.

5. Skip one stitch and then work a slip stitch into the next stitch of the previous row.

6. Work three chains.

7. Repeat steps 3–5 to complete a second picot.

8. Continue working stitches to the end of the row in the same manner.

Large picot edge

1. With the wrong side facing you, work a row of single crochet along the edge of the crocheted fabric. Make sure the number of stitches is a multiple of three plus two.

2. Turn your work and work one chain.

3. Work a single crochet into the next stitch of the previous row.

4. Work five chains.

5. Take the hook through the back of the fifth chain from the hook.

6. Wrap the yarn over the hook and pull through both loops on the hook to form a slip stitch.

7. Skip the next single crochet in the previous row and then work a single crochet into each of the next two stitches.

8. Repeat steps 4–7 to complete a second picot.

9. Continue working stitches to the end of the row in the same manner.

Blanket stitch

Blanket stitch can help to make an uneven edge appear straight.

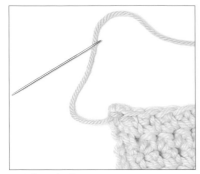

1. Thread the yarn into a tapestry needle and secure it on the back of the fabric.

2. Holding the fabric so the edge is at the bottom, bring the yarn to the front on the left-hand side through the space between the first and second stitches of the last row of crochet.

3. Take the needle, from front to back, through the space between the second and third stitches of the last row of crochet.

4. With the tip of the needle extending beyond the edge of the fabric, loop the yarn behind the needle tip.

5. Pull the yarn through until the loop lies against the emerging thread but does not distort it.

6. Work a second stitch between the third and fourth crochet stitches following steps 3–5.

7. Continue working stitches to the end of the row in the same manner.

8. After working the last stitch, flip the fabric over. Work two tiny back-stitches into the back of the last stitch to end off the yarn.

9. If you wish to work around a corner, work three stitches that all begin through the same hole in the fabric at the corner as shown.

Blocking

Blocking is the key to a beautiful finish to your crocheted project. It also helps the edges lie flat and makes it easier to join pieces. You will need a blocking board and long rustproof glass-headed or T pins. Blocking boards can be purchased from most needlework shops, but you can also make your own by covering a large piece of Styrofoam or cork with one or two layers of thin batting and then covering the batting with cotton check fabric.

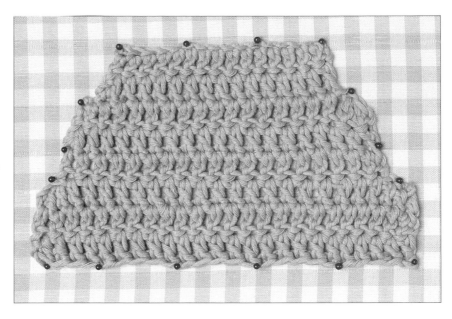

Place your crocheted piece or pieces onto your blocking board and pin them out to the measurements stated in your pattern. Use plenty of pins so you obtain nice straight edges.

If a piece is highly textured, place it face up onto the board; otherwise it doesn't really matter if it is faceup or facedown.

Use one of the following methods to complete the blocking process:

- Place a damp cloth over the piece. Press down lightly with your hands so some of the moisture is released into the crocheted piece. Leave until dry.

- Lightly mist the piece with a spray bottle of clean, cold water until it is slightly damp. Leave until dry.

- Place a pressing cloth over the piece. Using a warm steam iron, move it around approximately ⅜" to ¾" (1 to 2 cm) above the surface of the cloth until the steam has penetrated the crochet. Leave until dry.

- Place a damp pressing cloth over the piece. Using a warm, dry iron and a press-and-lift action, gently cover the whole cloth. Do not drag the iron back and forth across the cloth. Leave until dry. *Note: This method is not suitable for highly textured pieces.*

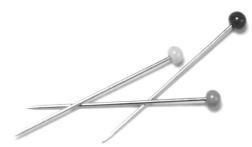

Joining pieces

Sewn Seams: Backstitch Work the seam 1 to 2 crochet stitches from the edge.

Backstitch creates a strong, firm seam suitable for loosely crocheted garments or where edges are uneven.

1. Place the two pieces to be joined right sides together. Placing pins at right angles to the edge, pin the two pieces together.

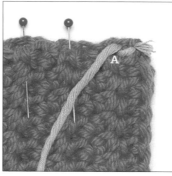

2. Thread the yarn through a tapestry needle. Secure the yarn at the right-hand end close to the edge (A).

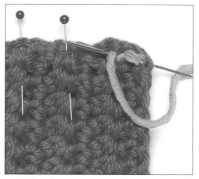

3. Take the yarn around the end and bring the needle out through the same hole in the fabric.

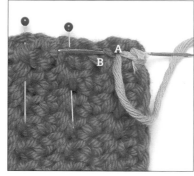

4. Pull the yarn firmly. Again, take the yarn around the end and bring the needle out just to the left of the previous stitch (B).

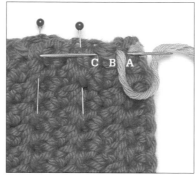

5. Pull the yarn through. Take the needle to the back at A and bring it out at C, on the other side of B.

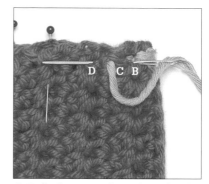

6. Pull the yarn through. Take the needle to the back at B and bring it out at D.

7. Pull the yarn through. Continue working stitches to the end of the seam in exactly the same manner.

8. Fasten off the yarn by working two tiny backstitches, one on top of the other.

HINTS
Sewn seams

Unless you have used a particularly bulky or textured yarn for the crochet, sew up the seam with the same yarn.

Sewn Seams: Chain stitch

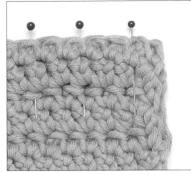

1. Place the two pieces to be joined right sides together. Placing pins at right angles to the edge, pin the two pieces together.

2. Thread the yarn through a tapestry needle. Secure the yarn at the right-hand end close to the edge (A). Take the yarn around the end and bring the needle out through the same hole.

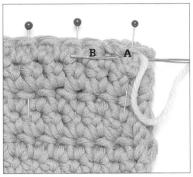

3. Pull the yarn firmly. Take the needle to the back at A and bring it out at B.

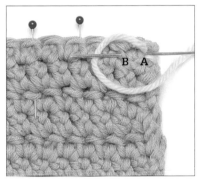

4. Loop the yarn so it is behind the tip of the needle.

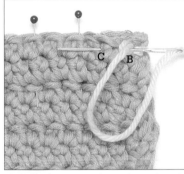

5. Pull the yarn through. Take the needle to the back at B and bring it out at C.

6. Again, loop the yarn so it is behind the tip of the needle and pull the yarn through to form a second stitch.

7. Continue working stitches to the end of the seam in exactly the same manner.

8. After working the last stitch, take the yarn around the end and bring it out through the last used hole.

9. Fasten off the yarn by working two tiny backstitches, one on top of the other.

Only use ladder
stitch when the two
edges you are joining
are straight and
contain the same
number of stitches
or rows.

Sewn Seams: Ladder stitch along top and bottom edges

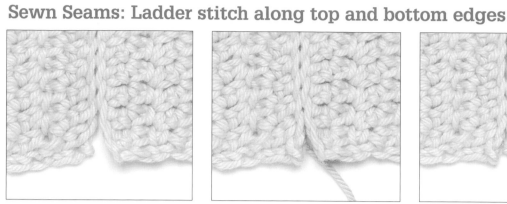

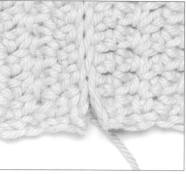

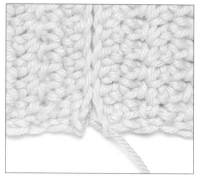

1. With right sides facing up, place the two pieces side by side so the stitches of the rows to be joined just touch.

2. Thread the yarn through a tapestry needle. Secure the yarn behind the first stitch on the lower edge of the left-hand piece.

3. Bring the yarn to the right side through the upper loop of the first stitch on the right-hand piece.

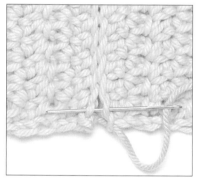

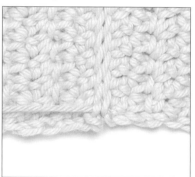

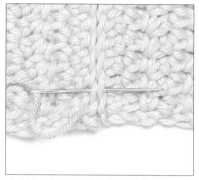

4. Take the needle, from right to left, behind the upper loop of the second stitch on the right-hand piece and the corresponding stitch on the left-hand piece.

5. Pull the yarn through.

6. Take the needle, from left to right, behind the upper loop of the next stitch on the left-hand piece and the corresponding stitch on the right-hand piece.

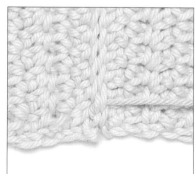

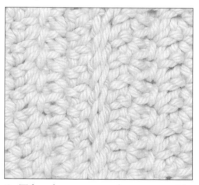

7. Pull the yarn through.

8. Continue working stitches back and forth across the two pieces in the same manner until you reach the end of the seam.

9. Take the yarn to the wrong side and fasten off by working two tiny backstitches, one on top of the other.

Finishing

152

Sewn Seams: Ladder stitch along side edges
This method is particularly suited to joining fabric made from long stitches.

1. With right sides facing up, place the two pieces side by side so the ends of the rows just touch.

2. Thread the yarn through a tapestry needle. Secure the yarn behind the first stitch on the lower edge of the left-hand piece.

3. Bring the yarn to the right side through the lower half of the first edge stitch on the left-hand piece.

4. Slide the needle, from bottom to top, behind the lower half of the first edge stitch on the right-hand piece.

5. Pull the yarn through.

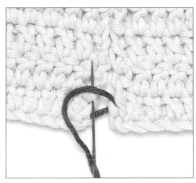

6. Slide the needle, from bottom to top, behind the upper half of the first edge stitch on the left-hand piece.

7. Pull the yarn through.

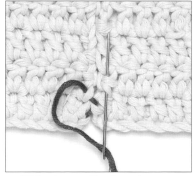

8. Slide the needle, from bottom to top, behind the lower half of the next edge stitch on the right-hand piece.

9. Pull the yarn through. Slide the needle, from bottom to top, behind the upper half of the next edge stitch on the left-hand piece.

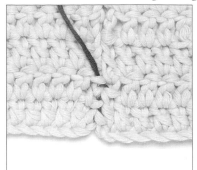

10. Pull the yarn through.

11. Continue working stitches back and forth across the two pieces in the same manner until you reach the end of the seam.

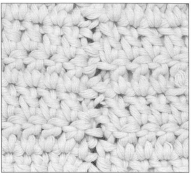

12. Take the yarn to the wrong side and fasten off by working two tiny back-stitches, one on top of the other.

Crocheted Seams: Slip stitch

This method creates a similar seam to the sewn chain-stitch seam (page 151).

HINTS
Crocheted seams

If you'd like your seam to be decorative, use a yarn that contrasts with your crocheted pieces.

Alternating slip stitch will produce the flattest of all the crocheted seams.

Single crochet creates a strong seam but it can be quite bulky.

You may find it easier to work the seam with a smaller hook than the one you used for the project.

1. Place the two pieces to be joined right sides together. Placing pins at right angles to the edge, pin the two pieces together.

2. Take the hook, from front to back, through both pieces. Wrap the yarn, from back to front, around the hook.

3. Pull the loop of yarn to the front.

4. Again, take the hook, from front to back, through both pieces approximately one crochet stitch to the left.

5. Loop the yarn over the hook as before.

6. Pull the loop through to the front and through the loop on the hook.

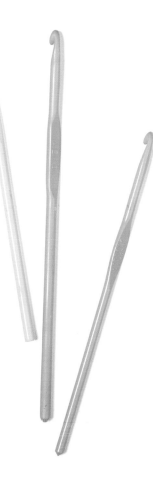

7. Repeat steps 4–6 until you reach the end of the seam.

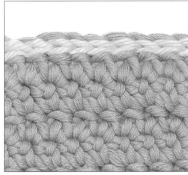

8. Fasten off the tails of yarn at each end following the instructions on page 24.

Crocheted Seams: Alternating slip stitch

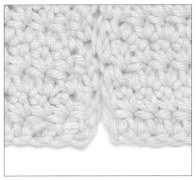

1. With wrong sides facing up, place the two pieces side by side so the ends of the rows just touch.

2. Take the hook, from front to back, through the lower left-hand corner of the right-hand piece.

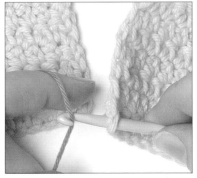

3. Wrap the yarn, from back to front, around the hook.

4. Pull the loop of yarn to the front.

5. Take the hook, from front to back, through the corresponding stitch on the left-hand piece.

6. Wrap the yarn as before and pull the loop through both the crocheted fabric and the loop on the hook to form a slip stitch.

7. Take the hook, from front to back, through the next stitch up on the right-hand piece.

8. Complete the slip stitch as before.

9. Take the hook, from front to back, through the corresponding stitch on the left-hand piece.

10. Complete the slip stitch as before.

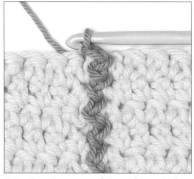

11. Continue working slip stitches up the seam in the same manner. Always alternate from side to side.

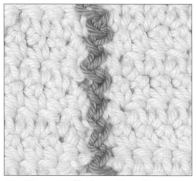

12. Fasten off the tails of yarn at each end following the instructions on page 24. On the right side of the fabric, the seam appears as a zigzag.

Finishing

Crocheted Seams: Single crochet along top and bottom edges

Place the pieces right sides together for an invisible seam, or wrong sides together for a decorative seam.

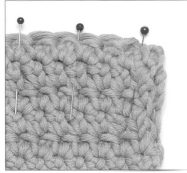

1. Place the two pieces to be joined together. Placing pins at right angles to the edge, pin the two pieces together.

2. Work a slipknot and place it on the hook. Hold the pieces of fabric in front of the working yarn.

3. Take the hook, from front to back, beneath the top of the first stitch on each piece.

4. Wrap the yarn, from back to front, around the hook.

5. Pull the loop of yarn to the front. There are two loops on the hook.

6. Complete the single crochet stitch.

7. Take the hook, from front to back, through the top of the next stitch on each piece.

8. Work a single crochet stitch.

9. Continue working single crochet across the top of the two pieces until you reach the end of the seam.

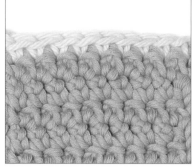

10. Fasten off the tails of yarn at each end following the instructions on page 24.

Seam worked with right sides of fabric together

Seam worked with wrong sides of fabric together

Crocheted Seams: Single crochet along side edges

Place the pieces right sides together for an invisible seam, or wrong sides together for a decorative seam.

1. Place the two pieces to be joined together. Placing pins at right angles to the edge, pin the two pieces together.

2. Work a slipknot and place it on the hook. Hold the pieces of fabric in front of the working yarn.

3. Take the hook, from front to back, through both pieces near the edge.

4. Work a single crochet stitch.

5. Continue working single crochet in the same manner to the end of the seam, spacing the stitches evenly.

6. Fasten off the tails of yarn at each end following the instructions on page 24.

Index